Quilt Batik!

Cheryl Brown

Martingale®
Create with Confidence

Dedication

To my amazing mom and dad, who have always
encouraged me to do my best and supported my
creative efforts. I love you!

Quilt Batik!

© 2012 by Cheryl Brown

Martingale®
19021 120th Ave. NE, Ste. 102
Bothell, WA 98011-9511 USA
ShopMartingale.com

Printed in China

17 16 15 14 13 12   8 7 6 5 4 3 2 1

Library of Congress Cataloging-in-Publication Data is
available upon request

ISBN: 978-1-60468-159-8

Mission Statement

Dedicated to providing quality products and
service to inspire creativity.

Credits

President & CEO: Tom Wierzbicki
Editor in Chief: Mary V. Green
Design Director: Paula Schlosser
Managing Editor: Karen Costello Soltys
Technical Editor: Ellen Pahl
Copy Editor: Melissa Bryan
Production Manager: Regina Girard
Illustrator: Christine Erikson
Cover Designer: Paula Schlosser
Text Designer: Connor Chin
Photographer: Brent Kane

Contents

4   Introduction

5   Batiks Q&A

The Quilts

11 September

19 Purple Daze

23 Reverse Psychology

29 Pastelmania

33 It's Hip to Be Square

37 Tangerine Summers

41 Winter Stars

49 Pink of Perfection

53 Simply Irresistible

57 Power to the People

65 Night and Day

77 Paradise Winds

80 About the Author

Introduction

When I was introduced to quiltmaking, one of the first projects I made was with batik fabrics. I have loved them ever since! I still have that first quilt, and I still display it in my living room. There is something rich and magical about the wonderful colors of batiks, and they make any project special.

In this book, I hope to share my love of batiks and perhaps shed some light on how to use them effectively. These designs would be fabulous in many different batik colorways, or even made with traditional quilting cotton. I hope to pass along some new ideas about how to put batiks together in a contemporary and fun way. As always, the joy of quilting comes from making each project your own. Use *your* favorite batiks to make your quilt unique. Enjoy the process, because that's why we quilt!

Batiks Q&A

We quilters love batiks, but how many of us know what's behind those gorgeous prints and how they came to be? This section will clear up some of the mystery of the batik-making process and provide a bit of historical background. I'll also delve into the exciting world of batik colorways and address some common questions you may have about using these fabulous fabrics.

What Is Batik?

Batik is a basic hand-dyeing method elevated to an art form. In this method, wax is used as a resist to create patterns on fabric. When dye is applied to the fabric, the areas coated with wax do not accept the color. The resulting fabric is characterized by a mottled or marbleized look, and can contain anywhere from one dye color to dozens. The fabric used to make batiks is usually much more tightly woven than traditional quilting fabric because it has to withstand the many dyeing steps it undergoes. The word *batik* comes from the Javanese *tik*, meaning "to dot."

What Is the History of Batiks?

The technique of making batiks by dye-resistant methods has been around for 2,000 years or more, and can be traced back to ancient Egypt and Asia. Early batiks were made of silk; cottons didn't come about until later. Some of the traditional patterns were used exclusively for royalty.

Batiks as we know them today, however, originated in Indonesia, primarily in Java and Bali. The art form spread to Europe through the settling of Indonesia, mainly by the Dutch. Merchants took Indonesian artisans to Holland to teach the Dutch how to make the exotic fabrics, and they even established some factories there. Later, copper *tjaps* (called "chops" in English), or blocks, came into use for applying the wax to the fabric in patterns. In the early 1900s, the Germans became the first to create batiks through mass production.

How Are Batiks Made?

Basically, there are three different methods used to create batiks. Sometimes more than one method will be used on a single fabric. All three methods start with a sodium silicate wash to make the fabric colorfast.

The first batik method is a basic marbled color application. Sometimes the fabric will be scrunched up to give it a more mottled look. The fabric is dipped into a vat to apply the color, and then it is hung on drying racks outdoors, where the natural sunlight makes the dye even more colorful. Trained artisans know just how to fold the yards of fabric when dipping it in the dye to achieve the look they want, and they can repeat the process to add as many colors as desired.

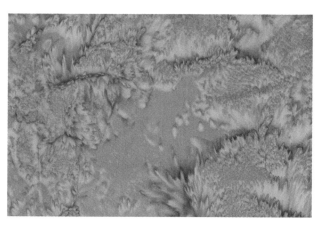

An example of vat-dyed batik.

The second batik method involves block printing or stamping to create a pattern on fabric. This technique uses a block called a chop that is made with strips of copper bent to create motifs and designs. The artisan dips the edges of the copper strips into hot wax and then, using his or her free arm as a guide, places the chop on the fabric to make waxed line "drawings" of the motifs.

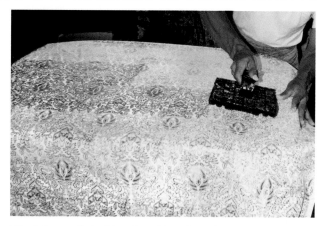

Wax being applied with a chop. Photo by Galen R Frysinger.

After the wax pattern is applied, the fabric will be dyed with the colors in the dye vats. The waxed area remains the original fabric color. Sometimes wax is applied after the fabric has been vat dyed one or more times. Each time, the newly waxed area will resist any additional dyes, while the new color will overdye the remainder of the fabric. The final step is a hot-water wash to remove the wax from the fabric. This method is limited to four colors.

An example of a block-print batik. Photo courtesy of Anthology Fabrics.

The third batik method is a hand-drawn technique in which the artisan uses hot wax and a stylus, called a *jhuning* (or "canting" in English), to create an original pattern on the fabric. Usually the artist will sketch the pattern with a pencil and then apply the wax on the drawn lines with the canting. Colored dyes are then applied individually using a brush, including the background colors. The fabric is then allowed to dry before going through the finishing process. This offers the advantage of being able to use more colors and have a much larger pattern surface, as the copper chops are typically only about 9" square. This method also allows the artisan to apply fine details to the design.

As with the chop method, the wax is removed from the fabric after the final dyeing step.

A close-up view of wax being applied with the canting. Photo courtesy of Anjie Davison at www.pompomemporium.com.

An example of a hand-drawn batik. Photo courtesy of Marjorie L. Claus, www.marjorieclaus.com.

What Are Batik Colorways?

The unique method of dyeing batiks makes the possible colorways endless! For your ease in using this book, I've chosen to categorize them into some basic groups of color and value.

First are my favorites—bright batiks. These are characterized by very vibrant saturations of color and can range from lime green to hot pink. They can be seen in "Power to the People" on page 58.

A range of bright batiks

Closely related to the brights are the jewel tones. They have fairly strong saturation, but are usually a little more subdued and are characterized by deep purples, blues, greens, and reds. This type of colorway can be seen in "Paradise Winds" on page 76.

Rich jewel-tone batiks

The next group I'll call earth tones. They're darker, more muted, and less saturated with color than the other groups. This is where I would categorize browns, tans, dark greens, and muted yellows. I've used this type of colorway in "Purple Daze" on page 18, although the jewel-tone category is represented by several of the batiks as well.

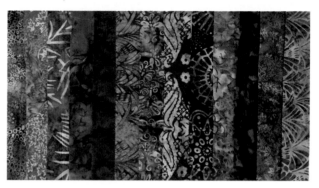

A grouping of batiks in earth tones

Pastels make up another group. These batiks have light saturations and values, and they include soft pinks, yellows, greens, and light violets. You can see them featured in "Pastelmania" on page 28.

Assorted pastel batiks

Fabrics in the group I call neutrals are characterized by their minimal amount of color. Light grays, off-whites, and tans in this category make wonderful backgrounds for the bolder colors. I've used neutrals in several of the quilts when I needed a background color to set off the blocks or appliqué. This group would also include blacks and whites. I used a variety of neutral batiks as the starting point in "Winter Stars" on page 42; "Reverse Psychology" on page 23 shows good examples of black and white batiks.

Neutral batiks with very little color

A number of specialty batiks incorporate different methods of creating the resist design areas. Striped batiks are one example. They add a lot of interest to a quilt design and make great borders and bindings, too. I used a wonderful stripe for the outer border in the quilt "Tangerine Summers" on page 36.

A selection of striped batiks

Another specialized technique involves using actual plants or leaves to create subtle botanical prints. The pieces of greenery are placed on the fabric during the drying process to produce areas that are lighter in color. I used a gorgeous dark-purple piece like this in the stars and border of "Purple Daze" on page 18.

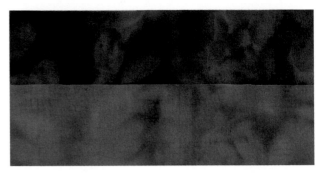

Leaf-print batiks

You'll also find quite a few batiks that are made as specialty prints. In the photograph below, I've included some with animal themes, Christmas themes, and even themes related to Alaska, thanks to my cute sister-in-law who found them while on vacation in that state. I used a fun batik printed with Christmas trees in the quilt "Winter Stars" on page 42.

Batiks in a variety of theme prints

How Do You Match Batiks?

Most batiks are multicolored, so matching them is actually very easy. I like to begin by choosing one batik that I absolutely love. Then I start pulling out other fabrics that have some of the same hues as the main batik, but fewer colors overall.

For a good example of how to develop a quilt around a basic batik color, check out "Pink of Perfection," shown in detail below and in full on page 48. I started with the fabulous pink-and-red leaf batik (used for the border and setting triangles) and built the color scheme around that fabric. Sometimes you'll find two or three batiks that look wonderful together, and then you can build on the general feel of all the fabrics, using some of the colorway groupings discussed previously.

Do You Sew Differently with Batiks?

I love to sew with batiks! Because batiks are made of tightly woven fabric, they fray very little when piecing. It's also very easy to press them crisply, so they look fabulous in pieced quilts. I don't machine piece any differently than with other quilting cottons, but I do use a new needle in the machine each time I begin a batik project. Because of their tight weave, batiks can be a little harder for the needle to pierce, so a sharp, new needle is best for stitching.

I also like to hand appliqué with batiks. Some people don't care for it because the fabric is a little stiff, but I think this gives a nice, crisp edge to the appliqué. Working with many layers is a challenge, however, since it can be difficult to get the needle through all the fabric. If I'm layering a design, I will appliqué the top piece to the next piece, and then layer downward as shown.

Stitch top layer to the layer beneath it.   Stitch combined layers to the next layer.

Stitch entire appliqué to background fabric.

To summarize, batiks are a lot of fun to work with and can make a traditional pattern more contemporary. Many companies manufacture fabulous batiks for quilting, and I always love finding a quilt store that has a good selection. The following websites are also useful resources:

- batikguild.org.uk
- bali-fabrics.com
- penangbatik.com.my
- anthologyfabrics.com

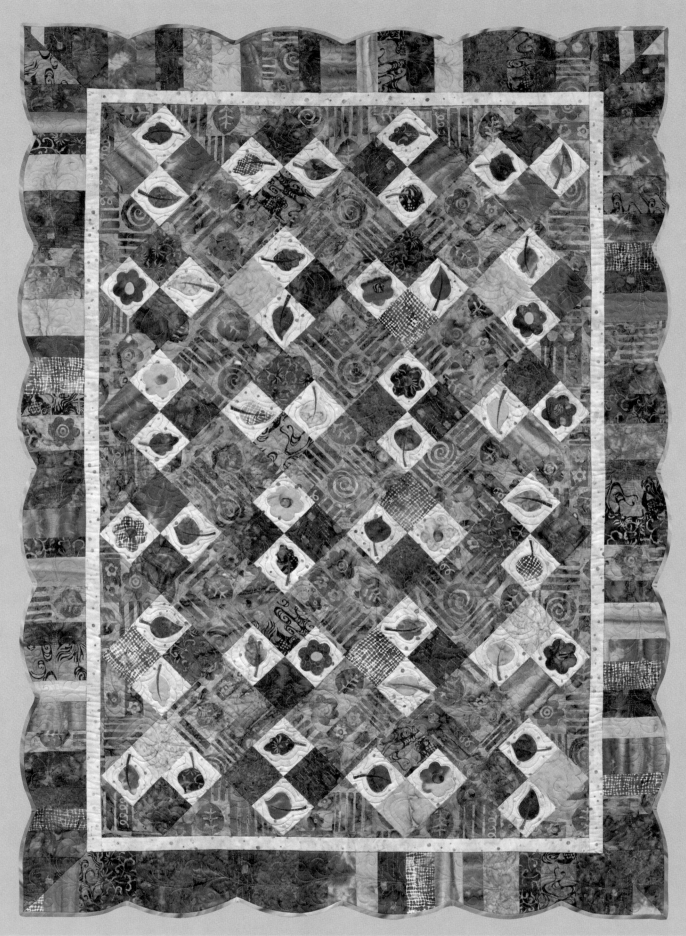

Finished Quilt: 45½" x 62½" | Finished Blocks: 6" x 6"

September

Materials

Yardage is based on 42"-wide fabric. Fat quarters measure 18" x 21".

1½ yards of orange-and-pink batik for large blocks, setting triangles, and outer border

⅞ yard of white polka-dot batik for appliqué block backgrounds and inner border

1 fat quarter *each* of 14 assorted earth-tone and bright batiks (green, orange, yellow, and pink) for Four Patch blocks and appliqués

¾ yard of orange-and-pink striped batik for binding

3 yards of fabric for backing

50" x 67" piece of batting

2 skeins of embroidery floss for leaf stems

Freezer paper

Light and dark marking pencils

Cutting

All measurements include ¼"-wide seam allowances.

From the white polka-dot batik, cut:
5 strips, 3½" x 42"; crosscut into 48 squares, 3½" x 3½"
5 strips, 1½" x 42"

From the 14 assorted batik fat quarters, cut a *total* of:
48 squares, 3½" x 3½"
22 to 24 random-width strips (1½" to 3" x 21"); crosscut into 5"-long rectangles

From the orange-and-pink batik, cut:
3 strips, 6½" x 42"; crosscut into 15 squares, 6½" x 6½"
4 squares, 9¾" x 9¾"; cut into quarters diagonally to yield 16 quarter-square triangles
2 squares, 5⅛" x 5⅛"; cut in half diagonally to yield 4 half-square triangles
3 or 4 random-width strips (1½" to 3" x 42"); crosscut into 5"-long rectangles

Appliquéd Blocks

The instructions are written for hand appliqué, but you can use your own favorite method if you prefer.

1 Using the leaf and flower patterns on page 17, trace the appliqué shapes onto the dull side of freezer paper and cut out each template on the drawn line. Make the quantity specified on the pattern for each shape.

2 Using the assorted earth-tone and bright batiks, press each freezer-paper template shiny side down onto the right side of the fabric and trace. The traced line will be your stitching line. Cut out each appliqué shape, adding a scant ¼" seam allowance around the marked lines. Gently peel the freezer paper off the fabric.

3 Position each leaf and flower in the middle of a white polka-dot 3½" square, making sure you have room for the stem, and hand appliqué in place. Position the flower centers on each flower and hand appliqué in place.

4 Mark the stem of each leaf with a light or dark pencil, depending on what will be easiest to see on the fabric. Referring to "Embroidery Stitches" at right and using two strands of contrasting embroidery floss, straight stitch the outline for each stem and use a satin stitch to fill in the center of each stem. Make 12 flower blocks and 36 leaf blocks (12 each of the three leaf patterns).

Block Assembly

1 Select two appliqué blocks and two assorted 3½" squares for each block, referring to the photo on page 10 for color-placement ideas.

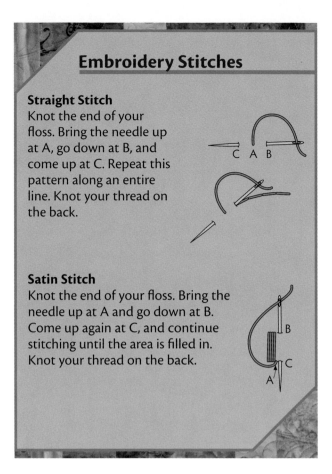

Embroidery Stitches

Straight Stitch
Knot the end of your floss. Bring the needle up at A, go down at B, and come up at C. Repeat this pattern along an entire line. Knot your thread on the back.

Satin Stitch
Knot the end of your floss. Bring the needle up at A and go down at B. Come up again at C, and continue stitching until the area is filled in. Knot your thread on the back.

2 Sew an appliqué block to each of the assorted squares as shown. Press seam allowances toward the assorted squares.

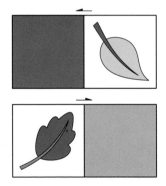

3 Sew the units from step 2 together as shown. Repeat to make 24 blocks.

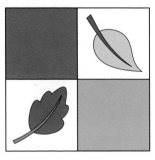

Make 24.

Quilt Top Assembly

1 Arrange the appliquéd blocks, the orange-and-pink 6½" squares, and the quarter-square and half-square triangles in diagonal rows as shown in the quilt assembly diagram at right. Note how the orientation of the appliqué blocks alternates so that in one block the flowers and leaves are at the top and bottom, while in the adjacent block they're on the left and right.

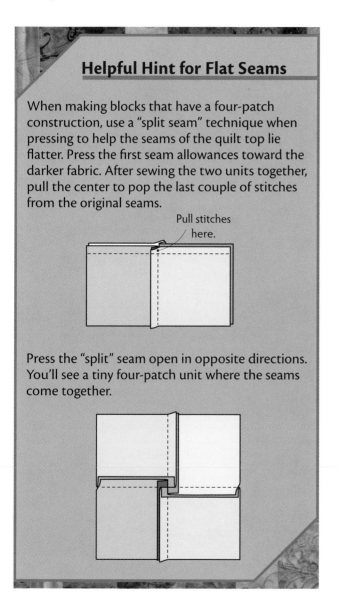

Helpful Hint for Flat Seams

When making blocks that have a four-patch construction, use a "split seam" technique when pressing to help the seams of the quilt top lie flatter. Press the first seam allowances toward the darker fabric. After sewing the two units together, pull the center to pop the last couple of stitches from the original seams.

Press the "split" seam open in opposite directions. You'll see a tiny four-patch unit where the seams come together.

2 Sew the blocks together into diagonal rows. Press the seam allowances toward the orange-and-pink squares. Sew the rows together, adding the corner triangles last; press.

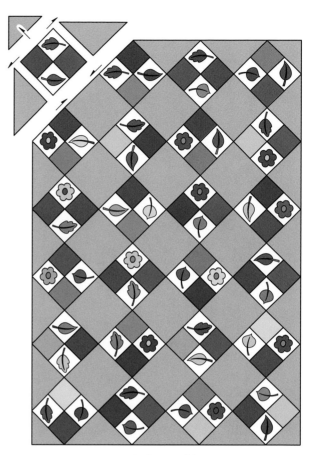

Quilt assembly

3 Sew the polka-dot 1½"-wide strips together end to end to make one long strip. Measure the width of the quilt through the center and cut two strips to this length. Sew the strips to the top and bottom of the quilt, and press toward the inner border. Measure the length through the center, including the borders just added, and cut strips for the sides of the quilt. Sew to the quilt and press.

4 Sew the 5"-long rectangles together on the long edges to make one strip at least 234" long.

5 Measure the length and width of the quilt through the center. Add 9" to the measured dimensions (finished width of the border x 2). From the pieced strip, cut two border strips for the top and bottom (quilt width + 9") and two border strips for the sides (quilt length + 9").

6 Use pins to mark the centers of the quilt edges and border strips. From the center pin in the border, measure out one half the finished length of the border and place a pin at each end to mark the point. Pin the strips to the quilt, matching the pins at the centers and matching the pins at the ends with the raw edge of the quilt. Sew the strips to the top and bottom and then the sides of the quilt, starting and stopping ¼" from the raw edges of the quilt on all sides.

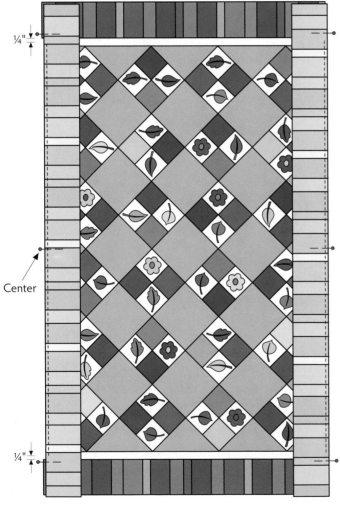

¼"

Center

¼"

Stitching begins and ends ¼"
from corner of the quilt top.

7 Fold the quilt diagonally, right sides together, and line up the edges of the border strips. Using a pencil and a ruler with a 45° angle printed on it, mark a 45° angle on the wrong side of each border strip, using your stitching line as a guide and starting at the intersection of the seam lines as shown.

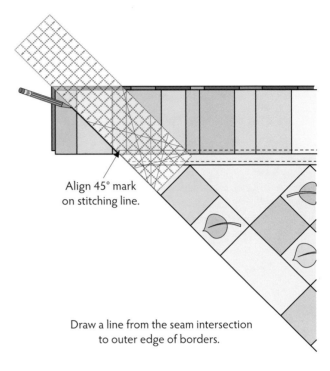

Align 45° mark
on stitching line.

Draw a line from the seam intersection
to outer edge of borders.

8 Pin carefully, matching the marked lines. Sew on the marked line. Backstitch at both ends. Trim the seam allowances to ¼" and press them open. Miter the remaining corners in the same manner.

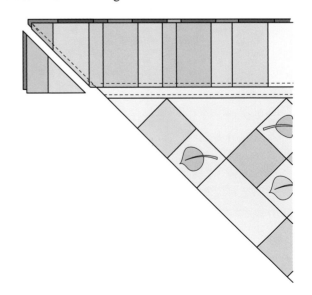

9 Make a scallop template using freezer paper and the scallop pattern on page 17. Starting at the center of one outer border, trace the scallop template using a dark marking pencil. The curved edge of the template should be aligned with the outer edge of the quilt. Mark six scallops on the top and bottom borders and eight scallops on the side borders. Leave the corners square. *Do not trim the scallops yet.* They will be cut after the quilting is finished.

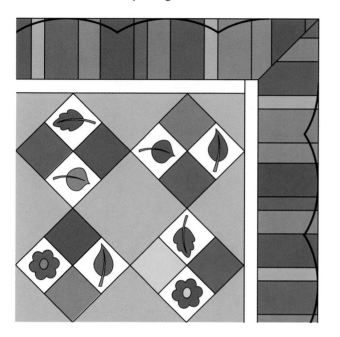

Finishing the Quilt

1 Prepare the backing fabric. Layer the backing, batting, and quilt top. Baste the layers together, and hand or machine quilt as desired. (If you are taking your quilt to a long-arm quilter, you don't need to baste the layers together.)

2 Cut the scallops carefully along the marked lines using good, sharp fabric scissors.

3 Cut and prepare approximately 260" of 2¼"-wide bias binding from the orange-and-pink striped batik.

4 Sew the binding to the quilt. To sew the inside points of the binding, stop ¼" from the inside point with the needle in the down position, and then pivot the quilt, fitting the binding to the inside corner and along the next curve.

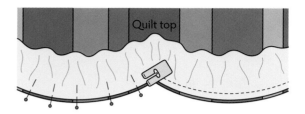

5 Continue sewing along each curve, pivoting at each inside point. Turn the binding to the back of the quilt, fitting it into each inside point. Hand stitch the binding in place as shown.

Quilting Suggestions

In the outer border I used a feather motif that curved with the scallops. In the center I used an allover pattern, outlining the leaves and flowers.

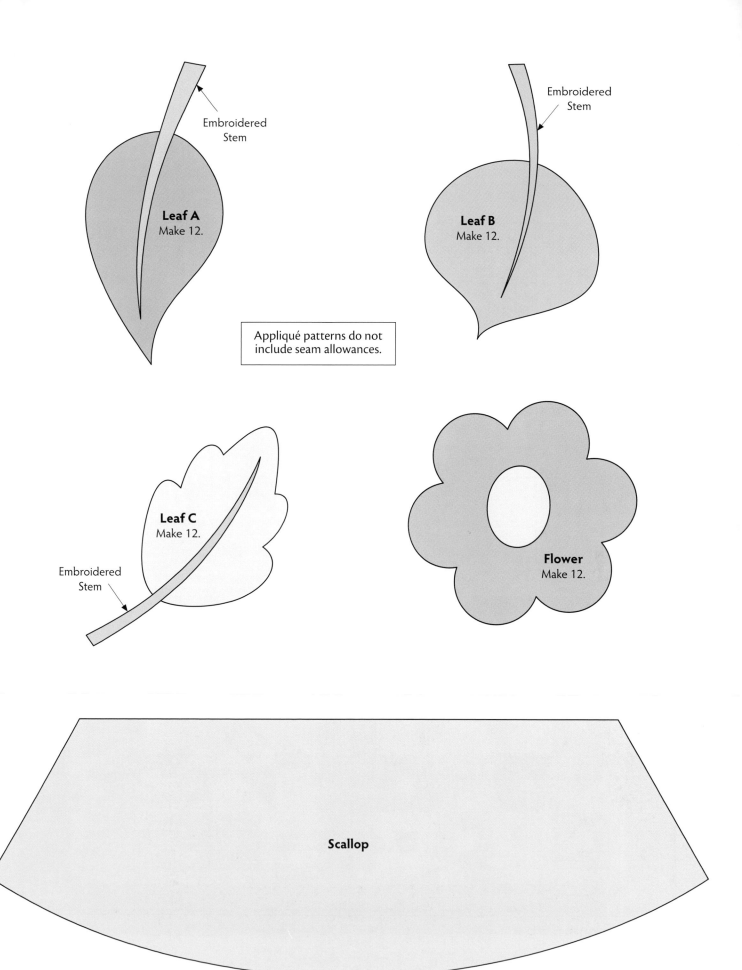

Embroidered Stem

Leaf A
Make 12.

Embroidered Stem

Leaf B
Make 12.

Appliqué patterns do not include seam allowances.

Leaf C
Make 12.

Embroidered Stem

Flower
Make 12.

Scallop

Finished Quilt: 67½" x 79½" | Finished Blocks: 6" x 6" and 18" x 18"

Purple Daze

Materials

Yardage is based on 42"-wide fabric.

2 yards of dark-purple batik for Star blocks and outer border

1½ yards of yellow-and-pink batik for Star block backgrounds

⅞ yard of beige batik for inner border and border corner blocks

40 precut 2½" x 42" strips of batiks for Square-in-a-Square blocks*

⅞ yard of purple-striped batik for binding

5¼ yards of fabric for backing**

72" x 84" piece of batting

Marking pencil

* *Bundles of precut strips go by various names, depending on the manufacturer; two popular options are Bali Pops by Hoffman Fabrics and Jelly Rolls by Moda.*

** *If the backing fabric is 42" wide after prewashing, 4 yards will be enough.*

Cutting

All measurements include ¼"-wide seam allowances.

From the precut batik strips, cut:

63 squares, 2½" x 2½"

63 matching sets of 2 squares, 2½" x 2½", and 2 rectangles, 2½" x 6½"

From the dark-purple batik, cut:

3 strips, 5⅜" x 42"; crosscut into 16 squares, 5⅜" x 5⅜"

1 strip, 5" x 42"; crosscut into 4 squares, 5" x 5"

1 strip, 3⅜" x 42"; crosscut into 8 squares, 3⅜" x 3⅜"

2 strips, 3⅛" x 42"; crosscut into 16 squares, 3⅛" x 3⅛"

6 strips, 5½" x 42"

From the yellow-and-pink batik, cut:

4 squares, 10¼" x 10¼"

1 strip, 5¾" x 42"; crosscut into 4 squares, 5¾" x 5¾"

2 strips, 5" x 42"; crosscut into 16 squares, 5" x 5"

2 strips, 2¾" x 42"; crosscut into 16 squares, 2¾" x 2¾"

From the beige batik, cut:

2 squares, 6¼" x 6¼"

1 strip, 5½" x 42"; crosscut into 4 squares, 5½" x 5½"

7 strips, 2" x 42"

I've heard it said that purple is the color of royalty. If I were a royal, I would want to wear this gorgeous shade of purple! This quilt includes wonderful Star blocks and the opportunity to use precut strips. If you love purple as much as I do, this project will put you in a daze!

Square-in-a-Square Block Assembly

Each block is made with two fabrics, one for the center square and a contrasting fabric for the outer squares and rectangles.

1 Sew matching 2½" squares to opposite sides of a 2½" center square; press seam allowances away from the center.

2 Sew matching 2½" x 6½" rectangles to the top and bottom as shown; press. Make 63 Square-in-a-Square blocks.

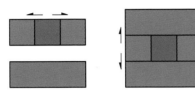

Make 63.

Star Block Assembly

1 Using a pencil and ruler, draw a diagonal line from corner to corner on the wrong side of each dark-purple 3⅛" square.

2 Lay two marked squares on opposite corners of a yellow-and-pink 5¾" square, right sides together. Sew ¼" from the drawn line on both sides. Cut on the drawn line; press.

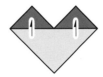

3 Lay a marked dark-purple square on the yellow-and-pink corner of each half from step 2, right sides together. Sew ¼" from the drawn line on both sides. Cut on the drawn line; press. This will give you four flying-geese units.

4 Sew flying-geese units to opposite sides of a dark-purple 5" square; press. Sew a yellow-and-pink 2¾" square to each end of the two remaining flying-geese units; press. Sew these units to the top and bottom of the block to make the center of the larger block.

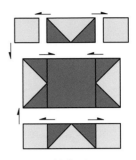

Make 4.

5 Using a pencil and ruler, draw a diagonal line from corner to corner on the wrong side of each dark-purple 5⅜" square. Lay two marked squares on opposite corners of a yellow-and-pink 10¼" square, right sides together. Sew ¼" from the drawn line on both sides. Cut on the drawn line; press.

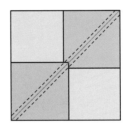
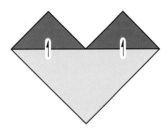

6 Lay a marked dark-purple square on the yellow-and-pink corner of each half from step 5, right sides together. Sew ¼" from the drawn line on both sides. Cut on the drawn line; press. This will give you four flying-geese units.

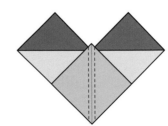

7 Sew flying-geese units to opposite sides of the block center; press. Sew a yellow-and-pink 5" square to each end of the two remaining flying-geese units; press. Sew these units to the top and bottom of the block. Make four Star blocks.

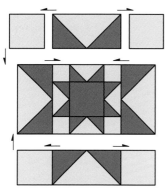

Make 4.

Pieced Outer Border

1 Using a pencil and ruler, draw a diagonal line from corner to corner on the wrong side of each dark-purple 3⅜" square. Lay two marked squares on opposite corners of a beige 6¼" square, right sides together. Sew ¼" from the drawn line on both sides. Cut on the drawn line; press.

2 Lay a marked dark-purple square on the beige corner of each half from step 1, right sides together. Sew ¼" from the drawn line on both sides. Cut on the drawn line; press. This will give you four flying-geese units. Make eight flying-geese units.

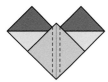

3 Sew the dark-purple 5½"-wide strips together end to end to make one long strip. Cut two strips, 52½" long, for the top and bottom borders and two strips, 64½" long, for the side borders.

4 Sew a flying-geese unit to each end of each border strip. Add a beige 5½" square to each end of the strips for the top and bottom borders.

Top and bottom borders

Side borders

Quilt Top Assembly

1 Arrange the blocks in rows and sections as shown in the quilt assembly diagram below, alternating light and dark blocks as much as possible. Sew the blocks together into sections, and then sew the sections together.

2 Sew the beige 2"-wide strips together end to end to make one long strip. Measure the width of the quilt through the center and cut two strips to that length. Sew the strips to the top and bottom of the quilt and press toward the border. Measure the length of the quilt, including the borders just added, and cut two strips to that length. Sew the strips to the sides of the quilt; press. The quilt should measure 57½" x 69½".

3 Sew the pieced outer-border strips to the sides and then to the top and bottom of the quilt; press.

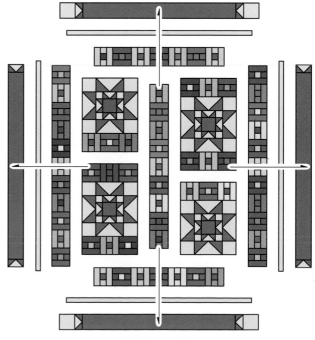

Quilt assembly

Finishing the Quilt

1 Prepare the backing fabric. Layer the backing, batting, and quilt top. Baste the layers together, and hand or machine quilt as desired. (If you are taking your quilt to a long-arm quilter, you don't need to baste the layers together.)

2 Cut and prepare approximately 310" of 2¼"-wide bias binding using the purple-striped batik. Sew the binding to the quilt.

Quilting Suggestions

In the border I machine quilted a C-shaped feather motif, and the same C-shaped swirl appears in the overall quilting in the center. For the stars, I stitched in the ditch around the outer and inner stars, plus I added one more layer of stitching inside the center square to echo the star shape. I used the C-shaped swirl in the inner star backgrounds, and treated the outer star backgrounds with the overall pattern.

Reverse Psychology

Materials

Yardage is based on 42"-wide fabric. Fat quarters measure 18" x 21".

2⅔ yards of black batik for blocks and outer border

2½ yards of white batik for blocks and outer border

1 fat quarter *each* of 10 assorted bright-green and yellow batiks for block centers, inner border, and binding*

5 yards of fabric for backing

64" x 82" piece of batting

* *You'll need ¾ yard of fabric for binding if you use just one fabric; then, 10 fat eighths (9" x 21" pieces) would be enough for block centers and inner border.*

Cutting

All measurements include ¼"-wide seam allowances.

From the black batik, cut:

5 strips, 1½" x 42"

5 strips, 1½" x 42"; crosscut into 34 rectangles, 1½" x 4½"

10 strips, 4½" x 42"

5 strips, 5½" x 42"

From the white batik, cut:

5 strips, 1½" x 42"

5 strips, 1½" x 42"; crosscut into 36 rectangles, 1½" x 4½"

10 strips, 4½" x 42"

4 strips, 5½" x 42"

From *each* of the 10 assorted fat quarters, cut:

2 strips, 2½" x 21"; crosscut into a total of 57 rectangles, 2½" x 4½"

1 strip, 6½" x 21"**

From the remainder of the 10 assorted fat quarters, cut a *total* of:

35 squares, 1½" x 1½"

** *This is for the pieced binding.*

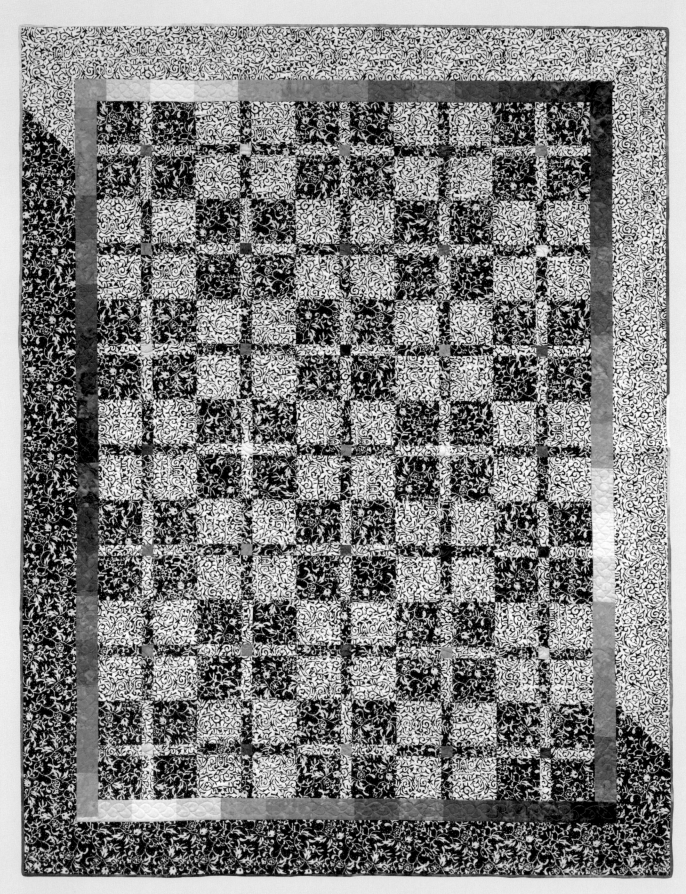

Finished Quilt: 59½" x 77½" | Finished Blocks: 9" x 9"

Block Assembly

1 Sew a black 4½"-wide strip to each long edge of a white 1½"-wide strip to make strip set A. Press the seam allowances toward the black fabric. Make five strip sets. Crosscut the strip sets into 36 segments, 4½" wide.

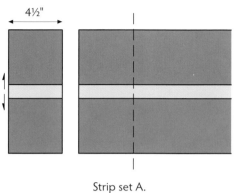

Strip set A.
Make 5. Cut 36 segments.

2 Sew white 1½" x 4½" rectangles to opposite sides of 18 of the assorted green and yellow 1½" squares to make unit B. Press the seam allowances toward the squares.

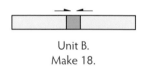

Unit B.
Make 18.

3 Sew strip set A segments to opposite sides of a unit B. Press the seam allowances toward the A segments. Make 18 dark blocks.

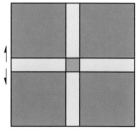

Make 18.

4 Sew a white 4½"-wide strip to each long edge of a black 1½"-wide strip to make strip set C. Press the seam allowances toward the black fabric. Make five strip sets. Crosscut the strip sets into 34 segments, 4½" wide.

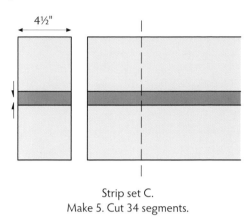

Strip set C.
Make 5. Cut 34 segments.

5 Sew black 1½" x 4½" rectangles to opposite sides of 17 of the assorted green and yellow 1½" squares to make unit D. Press the seam allowances toward the black fabric.

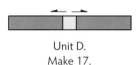

Unit D.
Make 17.

6 Sew strip set C segments to opposite sides of a unit D. Press the seam allowances toward unit D. Make 17 light blocks.

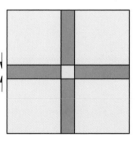

Make 17.

Quilt Top Assembly

1 Arrange the blocks in seven rows of five blocks each, starting with a dark block in the upper-left corner and alternating light and dark blocks as shown in the quilt assembly diagram on page 26.

2 Sew the blocks in each row together; press the seam allowances toward the dark blocks. Sew the rows together; press the seam allowances in one direction. The quilt top should measure 45½" x 63½".

3   Arrange the assorted green and yellow 2½" x 4½" rectangles from light to dark, and then back to light. See the quilt photo on page 24 for color-placement guidance. Sew the rectangles together end to end to make one long strip.

4   The inner borders will be cut and sewn one after the other, keeping the colors in order. This way the colors will flow around the quilt from light to dark and back again. Cut the bottom border 47½" long. Align the edge of the border with the lower-left corner of the quilt. Begin sewing about 6" from the lower-right corner of the quilt and sew to the left corner. This creates a partial seam that will be completed after the fourth border is added. Press the seam allowances toward the inner border.

5   Beginning with the end you cut in step 4, cut the left side border 65½" long. Sew it to the left side of the quilt and press.

6   Repeat to cut the top border 47½" long and sew it to the top of the quilt. Press. Cut the right side border 65½" long. Sew it to the right side of the quilt and press.

7   Complete the partial seam at the bottom of the quilt.

8   Sew the white 5½"-wide strips together end to end to make one long strip. Cut the top border 59½" long. Sew the black 5½"-wide strips together end to end to make one long strip. Cut the bottom border 59½" long.

9   To make the left side border, cut a black 70½"-long strip and a white 12½"-long strip. Lay the white strip at the top of the black strip at a 90° angle and use a pencil to mark a diagonal line from corner to corner. Sew on the line. Trim the seam allowances to ¼"; press the seam allowances toward the black fabric.

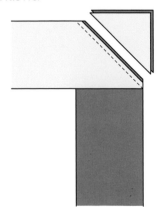

10   To make the right side border, cut a white 66½"-long strip and a black 16½"-long strip. Lay the black strip at the bottom of the white strip at a 90° angle and use a pencil to mark a diagonal line from corner to corner. Sew on the line. Trim the seam allowances to ¼"; press the seam allowances toward the black fabric.

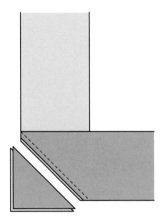

11   To add the mitered borders, refer to page 14 for steps 6–8 of "Quilt Top Assembly" for the quilt "September." Sew the white strip to the top of the quilt and the black strip to the bottom of the quilt. Sew the left and right side borders to the quilt; miter each corner.

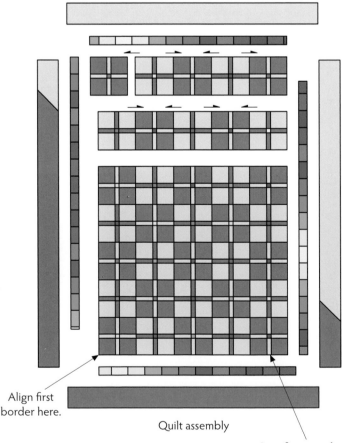

Align first border here.

Quilt assembly

Start first seam here. Finish seam after the other borders are sewn on.

Finishing the Quilt

1 Prepare the backing fabric. Layer the backing, batting, and quilt top. Baste the layers together, and hand or machine quilt as desired. (If you are taking your quilt to a long-arm quilter, you don't need to baste the layers together.)

2 To make the pieced binding, arrange the yellow and green 6½"-wide strips from light to dark. Sew the strips together in order, side by side.

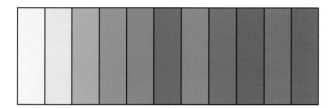

3 Cut 2¼"-wide bias strips from the pieced fabric. Sew the strips together in an alternating fashion so that the color will vary all the way around the quilt. Prepare approximately 300" of binding and sew the binding to the quilt.

Quilting Suggestions

In the border I machine quilted a swirly motif, which I modified as an allover pattern for the center of the quilt. In the inner border I used a loop motif.

Finished Quilt: 61¾" x 84½" | Finished Blocks: 8" x 8"

Pastelmania

These soft pastels bring to mind sunny days and warm breezes. Then when the sun goes down giving way to a cool summer night, I want to throw the quilt over myself while relaxing in a porch swing! Precut strips make this project extra quick and easy.

Materials

Yardage is based on 42"-wide fabric. Fat quarters measure 18" x 21".

1⅞ yards of blue tone-on-tone batik for pieced setting triangles, inner borders, and binding

1 yard of pastel batik for outer border

1 fat quarter *each* of 6 or 7 assorted pastel batiks for blocks and setting triangles

40 precut 2½" x 42" strips of pastel batiks for blocks and pieced border*

5 yards of fabric for backing

66" x 89" piece of batting

* *Bundles of precut strips go by various names, depending on the manufacturer; two popular options are Bali Pops by Hoffman Fabrics and Jelly Rolls by Moda.*

Cutting

All measurements include ¼"-wide seam allowances.

From the blue tone-on-tone batik, cut:

13 strips, 1½" x 42"

7 strips, 2" x 42"; crosscut into:

16 rectangles, 2" x 12⅝"

4 rectangles, 2" x 5⅛"

4 rectangles, 2" x 6⅝"

From the assorted pastel fat quarters, cut a *total* of:

9 squares, 8½" x 8½"

4 squares, 9⅝" x 9⅝"; cut into quarters diagonally to yield 16 quarter-square triangles

2 squares, 3⅝" x 3⅝"; cut in half diagonally to yield 4 half-square triangles

From the pastel batik, cut:

7 strips, 4½" x 42"

Pieced Blocks and Setting Triangles

1 Randomly select four 2½"-wide precut strips and sew them together along the long edges to make a strip set; press. Make 10. Crosscut each strip set into three squares, 8½" wide, for blocks, and three segments, 2½" wide. Cut one extra 2½"-wide segment from one strip set. Set the 2½" segments aside for the pieced border.

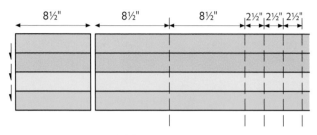

Make 10 strip sets.
Cut 30 squares. Cut 31 border units.

2 Trim each blue tone-on-tone 2" x 12⅝" rectangle on both ends at a 45° angle from the bottom corners as shown. Sew a trimmed rectangle to the long edge of each pastel quarter-square triangle, offsetting the corners as shown. Make 16.

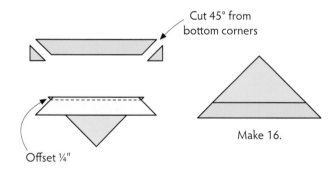

Cut 45° from bottom corners

Offset ¼"

Make 16.

3 Trim each blue tone-on-tone 2" x 5⅛" rectangle on one end at a 45° angle from the corner as shown. Sew to the left side of each pastel half-square triangle as shown.

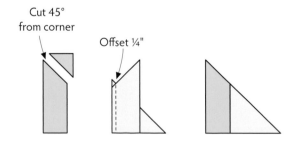

Cut 45° from corner

Offset ¼"

4 Trim each blue tone-on-tone 2" x 6⅝" rectangle on one end at a 45° angle from the corner as shown. Sew to the bottom of each pastel half-square-triangle unit as shown. Make four.

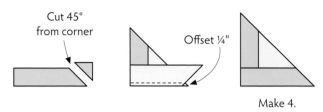

Cut 45° from corner

Offset ¼"

Make 4.

Quilt Top Assembly

1 Arrange the pieced blocks, the pastel 8½" squares, and the pieced setting triangles in diagonal rows as shown on the facing page. Note the differing orientation of the pieced blocks within each diagonal row.

2 Sew the pieces together into diagonal rows. Press the seam allowances toward the sides without seams. Sew the rows together, adding the corner triangles last; press.

3 Sew six of the blue tone-on-tone 1½"-wide strips together end to end to make one long strip. Measure the width of the quilt through the center and cut two strips to that length. Sew the strips to the top and bottom of the quilt and press toward the inner border. Measure the length of the quilt through the center, cut two strips to that length, and sew them to the sides of the quilt.

4 Sew the 2½"-wide segments from the pieced blocks together end to end to make one long strip. Measure, cut, and sew the strips to the top and bottom and then to the sides of the quilt as in step 3.

5 Sew the remaining blue tone-on-tone 1½"-wide strips together end to end to make one long strip. Measure, cut, and sew the strips to the top and bottom and then to the sides of the quilt for the second inner border.

6 Sew the pastel 4½"-wide strips together end to end to make one long strip. Measure, cut, and sew as before to add the outer-border strips to the top and bottom and then to the sides of the quilt.

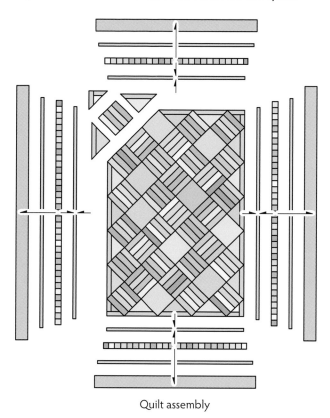

Quilt assembly

Finishing the Quilt

1 Prepare the backing fabric. Layer the backing, batting, and quilt top. Baste the layers together, and hand or machine quilt as desired. (If you are taking your quilt to a long-arm quilter, you don't need to baste the layers together.)

2 Cut and prepare approximately 310" of 2¼"-wide bias binding using the blue tone-on-tone batik. Sew the binding to the quilt.

Quilting Suggestions

I machine quilted a simple feather in the outer border, and stitched in the ditch of the inner borders. I added a crosshatch through the squares of the pieced border. On the inner areas of the quilt I used a floral motif complete with swirls, feathers, flowers, and leaves.

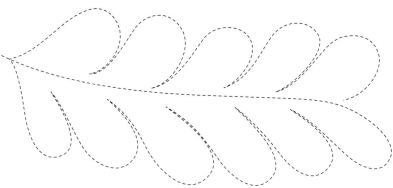

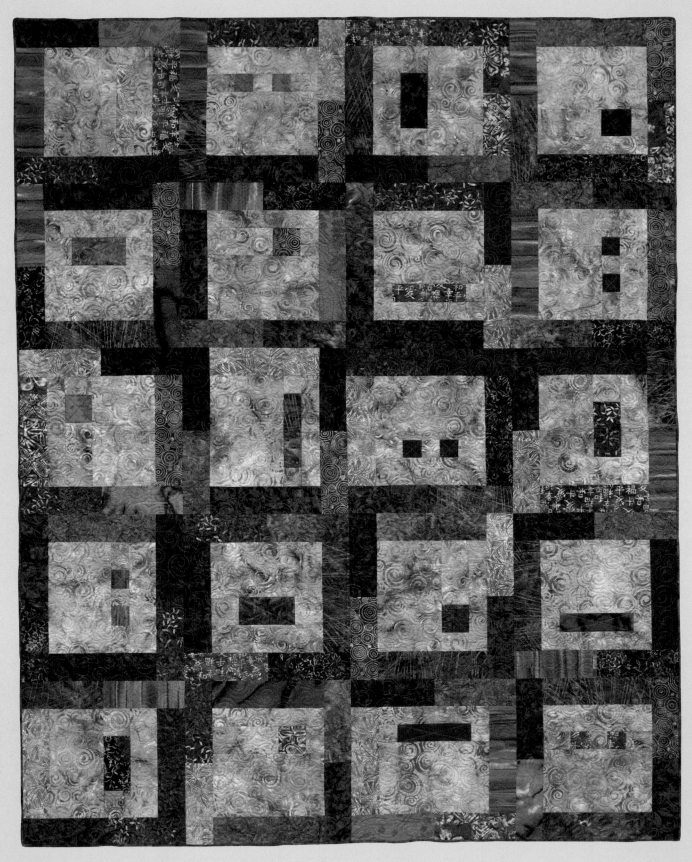

Finished Quilt: 72½" x 90½" | Finished Blocks: 18" x 18"

It's Hip to Be Square

Materials

Yardage is based on 42"-wide fabric. Fat quarters measure 18" x 21".

3⅛ yards of gray-and-tan batik for blocks

1 fat quarter *each* of 16 to 18 assorted jewel-tone batiks (green, purple, blue, and burgundy) for block centers and block borders

¾ yard of purple tone-on-tone batik for binding

5¾ yards of fabric for backing

77" x 95" piece of batting

Cutting

All measurements include ¼"-wide seam allowances.

From the gray-and-tan batik, cut:
  7 strips, 2½" x 42"; crosscut into:
    15 squares, 2½" x 2½"
    15 rectangles, 2½" x 3½"
    10 rectangles, 2½" x 12½"
  6 strips, 3½" x 42"; crosscut into:
    10 squares, 3½" x 3½"
    5 rectangles, 3½" x 7½"
    10 rectangles, 3½" x 12½"
  2 strips, 6½" x 42"; crosscut into 5 rectangles, 6½" x 12½"
  4 strips, 7½" x 42"; crosscut into 10 rectangles, 7½" x 12½"
  2 strips, 8½" x 42"; crosscut into 5 rectangles, 8½" x 12½"

From the assorted jewel-tone fat quarters, cut a *total* of:
  5 pairs of matching squares, 2½" x 2½"
  5 rectangles, 2½" x 8½"
  5 squares, 3½" x 3½"
  5 rectangles, 3½" x 6½"
  80 rectangles, 3½" x 9½"
  40 rectangles, 3½" x 12½"

Squares, squares, squares, and a few rectangles—that's what this quilt has, as well as some wonderful jewel-tone batiks. Each block has its own border, so in the end it's very simple to assemble the blocks for a great, contemporary look. This quilt will have you saying, "It's hip to be square!"

Block A Assembly

1 Sew a gray-and-tan 2½" square to each end of an assorted 2½" x 8½" rectangle. Press the seam allowances toward the gray-and-tan squares.

2 Sew a gray-and-tan 2½" x 12½" rectangle to the left side of the step 1 unit, and then sew a gray-and-tan 8½" x 12½" rectangle to the right side of the unit. Press the seam allowances toward the gray-and-tan rectangles. Make five blocks.

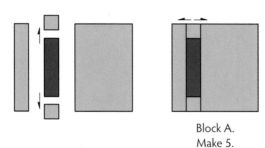

Block A.
Make 5.

Block B Assembly

1 Sew a gray-and-tan 2½" x 3½" rectangle to the top of an assorted 3½" square. Then sew a gray-and-tan 3½" x 7½" rectangle to the bottom of the square. Press the seam allowances toward the gray-and-tan rectangles.

2 Sew a gray-and-tan 2½" x 12½" rectangle to the left side of the step 1 unit. Then sew a gray-and-tan 7½" x 12½" rectangle to the right side of the unit. Press the seam allowances toward the gray-and-tan rectangles. Make five blocks.

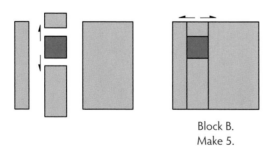

Block B.
Make 5.

Block C Assembly

1 Sew a gray-and-tan 3½" square to each end of an assorted 3½" x 6½" rectangle. Press the seam allowances toward the gray-and-tan squares.

2 Sew a gray-and-tan 3½" x 12½" rectangle to the left side of the step 1 unit. Then sew a gray-and-tan 6½" x 12½" rectangle to the right side of

the unit. Press the seam allowances toward the gray-and-tan rectangles. Make five blocks.

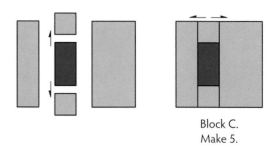

Block C.
Make 5.

Block D Assembly

1 Sew one of the assorted 2½" squares to the top of a gray-and-tan 2½" square. Then sew the matching 2½" square to the bottom of the square.

2 Sew gray-and-tan 2½" x 3½" rectangles to the top and bottom of the step 1 unit. Press the seam allowances toward the gray-and-tan pieces.

3 Sew a gray-and-tan 3½" x 12½" rectangle to the left side of the unit. Then sew a gray-and-tan 7½" x 12½" rectangle to the right side of the unit. Press the seam allowances toward the gray-and-tan rectangles. Make five blocks.

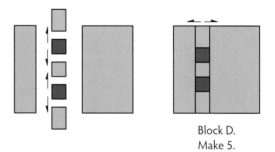

Block D.
Make 5.

Block Borders

1 Sew assorted 3½" x 12½" rectangles to the top and bottom of each block. Rotate the blocks so that the squares and rectangles are in different positions. Press the seam allowances toward the border.

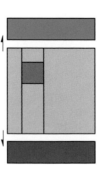

2 Pairing colors randomly, sew two of the assorted 3½" x 9½" rectangles together along the short ends. Press the seam allowances to one side. Make 40 side borders.

3 Sew the borders from step 2 to the sides of each block. Press the seam allowances outward.

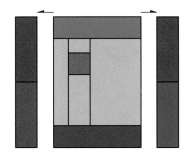

Quilt Top Assembly

1 Arrange the blocks in five rows of four blocks each, rotating the blocks so that the borders with seams are adjacent to borders without seams. The squares and rectangles within the blocks should be in different positions as shown in the quilt assembly diagram below. Refer also to the photo on page 32 for placement guidance.

2 Sew the blocks in each row together; press the seam allowances toward the borders with two pieces. Sew the rows together; press the seam allowances in one direction.

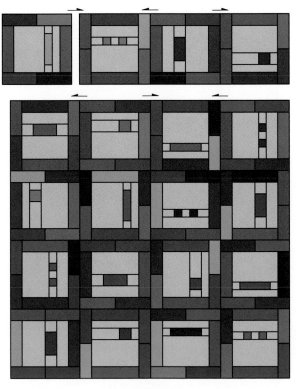

Quilt assembly

Finishing the Quilt

1 Prepare the backing fabric. Layer the backing, batting, and quilt top. Baste the layers together, and hand or machine quilt as desired. (If you are taking your quilt to a long-arm quilter, you don't need to baste the layers together.)

2 Cut and prepare approximately 340" of 2¼"-wide bias binding using the purple tone-on-tone batik. Sew the binding to the quilt.

Quilting Suggestions

For this graphic quilt, I kept the quilting simple by machine stitching an overall swirly motif.

Finished Quilt: 60½" x 72½" | Finished Blocks: 12" x 12"

Tangerine Summers

Materials

Yardage is based on 42"-wide fabric. Fat quarters measure 18" x 21".

1⅓ yards of yellow-and-orange striped batik for outer border
½ yard of dark-green batik for inner border and border corner blocks
1 fat quarter *each* of 10 assorted green batiks for blocks
1 fat quarter *each* of 10 assorted orange batiks for blocks
¾ yard of green-striped batik for binding
3¾ yards of fabric for backing
65" x 77" piece of batting
Marking pencil

Cutting

All measurements include ¼"-wide seam allowances.

From *each* of the green fat quarters, cut:
3 strips, 2⅞" x 21"; crosscut into 18 squares, 2⅞" x 2⅞"
1 square, 8⅞" x 8⅞"
2 squares, 2½" x 2½"

From *each* of the orange fat quarters, cut:
3 strips, 2⅞" x 21"; crosscut into 18 squares, 2⅞" x 2⅞"
1 square, 8⅞" x 8⅞"
2 squares, 2½" x 2½"

From the yellow-and-orange striped batik, cut:
2 strips, 1½" x 42"; crosscut into:
    8 rectangles, 1½" x 3½"
    8 rectangles, 1½" x 5½"
2 squares, 3⅞" x 3⅞"
6 strips, 5½" x 42"

From the dark-green batik, cut:
2 squares, 3⅞" x 3⅞"
6 strips, 1½" x 42"

I've always wanted to make a quilt using lime green and orange, and where else would you find such vibrant greens and oranges than in batiks? This sizzling quilt also uses one of my favorite blocks, a Framed Squares variation. It makes me think of eating orange sherbet on a summer afternoon. Yum!

Block Assembly

The instructions are written for making two blocks at a time. This will use all of the squares cut from one green and one orange fabric.

1 Using a pencil and ruler, draw a diagonal line from corner to corner on the wrong side of an orange 8⅞" square. Place the square on a green 8⅞" square, right sides together. Sew ¼" from the drawn line on both sides. Cut on the drawn line to create two block centers. Press the seam allowances toward the green halves.

2 Using a pencil and ruler, draw a diagonal line from corner to corner on the wrong side of the orange 2⅞" squares. Place a marked square on a green 2⅞" square, right sides together. Sew ¼" from the drawn line on both sides. Cut on the drawn line. Press the seam allowances toward the green halves. Make a total of 36, for 18 per block.

Speedy Half-Square Triangles

There are several paper products on the market for making half-square-triangle units. They are printed with the sewing and cutting lines, and the paper is removed from the back of the half-square-triangle units after sewing and cutting. I always use these when I have a lot of half-square-triangle units to make because they can save quite a bit of time.

3 Sew together four of the half-square-triangle units from step 2 as shown. Press the seam allowances toward the green fabric. *Make sure the triangles are pointing in the correct direction.* Make two. This is unit A.

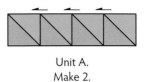

Unit A.
Make 2.

4 Sew together five units oriented in the opposite way as shown. *Make sure the triangles are pointing in the correct direction.* Then sew an orange 2½" square to the left end of the unit. Press the seam allowances toward the green fabric. This is unit B.

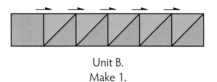

Unit B.
Make 1.

5 Sew together five units as shown. *Make sure the triangles are pointing in the correct direction.* Then sew a green 2½" square to the right end of the unit. Press the seam allowances toward the green fabric. This is unit C.

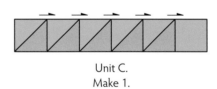

Unit C.
Make 1.

6 Sew A units to the top and bottom of the block center as shown. Press the seam allowances toward the block center. Sew a unit B to the right side of the block and a unit C to the left side of the block. Press the seam allowances toward the block center. Make a total of 20 blocks.

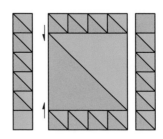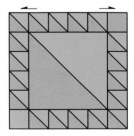

Make 20.

Border Corner Block Assembly

1 Using a pencil and ruler, draw a diagonal line from corner to corner on the wrong side of the yellow-and-orange striped 3⅞" squares. Place each marked square on a dark-green 3⅞" square, right sides together. Sew ¼" from the drawn line on both sides. Cut on the drawn line. Press the seam allowances toward the green halves. Make four half-square-triangle units.

2 Sew yellow-and-orange striped 1½" x 3½" rectangles to the top and bottom of each half-square-triangle unit. Press the seam allowances toward the striped fabric. Then sew yellow-and-orange 1½" x 5½" rectangles to opposite sides. Press the seam allowances toward the striped fabric.

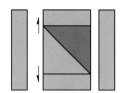

Make 4.

Quilt Top Assembly

1 Arrange the blocks in five rows of four blocks each, rotating each block so that the green and orange 2½" squares form a four-patch unit at every other corner, as shown in the quilt assembly diagram at right. Sew the blocks in each row together. Press the seam allowances toward the green corner squares. Sew the rows together. Press the seam allowances in one direction. The quilt top should measure 48½" x 60½".

2 Sew the dark-green 1½"-wide strips together end to end to make one long strip for the inner borders. Cut two strips, 60½" long, and sew them to the sides of the quilt. Press the seam allowances toward the inner border. Cut two border strips, 50½" long, and sew them to the top and bottom of the quilt. Press.

3 Sew the 5½"-wide yellow-and-orange stripe strips together end to end to make one long strip. Cut two border strips, 62½" long. Sew the strips to the sides of the quilt. Press the seam allowances toward the dark-green inner border.

4 Cut two striped border strips, 50½" long. Sew a corner block to each end of each strip, rotating the triangle so that it points outward in each corner as shown. Press the seam allowances toward the block. Sew the strips to the top and bottom of the quilt. Press the seam allowances toward the dark-green inner border.

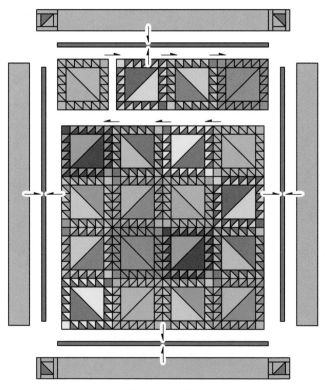

Quilt assembly

Finishing the Quilt

1 Prepare the backing fabric. Layer the backing, batting, and quilt top. Baste the layers together, and hand or machine quilt as desired. (If you are taking your quilt to a long-arm quilter, you don't need to baste the layers together.)

2 Cut and prepare approximately 280" of 2¼"-wide bias binding using the green-striped batik. Sew the binding to the quilt.

Quilting Suggestions

I machine quilted a groovy feather motif in the outer border, stitching in the ditch around the green triangle in each corner. I also stitched in the ditch along the inner border. In the center I quilted an overall pattern—a modified Baptist fan motif.

Winter Stars

Materials

Yardage is based on 42"-wide fabric. Fat quarters measure 18" x 21".

4½ yards of navy-blue tree-print batik for blocks and border

1⅔ yards of cream polka-dot batik for sashing strips

¾ yard of light-blue tone-on-tone batik for sashing star points

1 fat quarter *each* of 5 or 6 assorted gray and cream batiks for blocks and sashing squares

¾ yard of dark-blue batik for binding

5½ yards of fabric for backing

72" x 94" piece of batting

Marking pencil

You'll be walking in a winter wonderland with this fun tree-print batik! Since the fabric has a navy-blue background, I thought it needed sparkling stars to evoke the quiet and soft-ness of walking on freshly fallen snow on a clear winter's night.

Cutting

All measurements include ¼"-wide seam allowances.

From the assorted gray and cream fat quarters, cut a *total* of:
6 strips, 2½" x 21"; crosscut into 48 squares, 2½" x 2½"

From the navy-blue tree print, cut:
6 strips, 1½" x 42"; crosscut into 24 rectangles, 1½" x 9½", and 4 squares, 1½" x 1½"

4 strips, 3½" x 42"; crosscut into 44 squares, 3½" x 3½"

1 strip, 3⅞" x 42"; crosscut into 6 squares, 3⅞" x 3⅞"

1 strip, 4¼" x 42"; crosscut into 8 squares, 4¼" x 4¼". Cut into quarters diagonally to yield 32 quarter-square triangles.

1 strip, 2¾" x 42"; crosscut into 12 squares, 2¾" x 2¾"

1 strip, 3⅛" x 42"; crosscut into 12 squares, 3⅛" x 3⅛." Cut in half diagonally to yield 24 half-square triangles.

1 strip, 3¼" x 42"; crosscut into 7 squares, 3¼" x 3¼"

4 strips, 4½" x 42"

From the remaining navy-blue tree print, cut on the *lengthwise* grain:
2 strips, 4½" x 83"

From the remaining navy-blue tree print, cut on the *crosswise* grain:
7 strips, 9½" x 31"; crosscut into 21 squares, 9½" x 9½"

From the light-blue tone-on-tone batik, cut:
13 strips, 1½" x 42"; crosscut into 328 squares, 1½" x 1½"

2 strips, 1⅞" x 42"; crosscut into 28 squares, 1⅞" x 1⅞"

Continued on page 43.

Finished Quilt: 67½" x 89½" | Finished Blocks: 9" x 9"

From the cream polka-dot batik, cut:
21 strips, 2½" x 42"; crosscut into 82 rectangles, 2½" x 9½"

For 1 Star Block A (Cut 3 total.)

From one gray or cream batik, cut:
1 square, 3½" x 3½"

From a second gray or cream batik, cut:
2 squares, 3⅞" x 3⅞"

For 1 Star Block B (Cut 4 total.)

From one gray or cream batik, cut:
1 square, 3½" x 3½"
1 square, 4¼" x 4¼"; cut into quarters diagonally to yield 4 quarter-square triangles

From a second gray or cream batik, cut:
2 squares, 3⅞" x 3⅞"; cut in half diagonally to yield 4 half-square triangles

For 1 Star Block C (Cut 4 total.)

From one gray or cream batik, cut:
1 square, 3½" x 3½"
2 squares, 4¼" x 4¼"; cut into quarters diagonally to yield 8 quarter-square triangles

From a second gray or cream batik, cut:
1 square, 4¼" x 4¼"; cut into quarters diagonally to yield 4 quarter-square triangles

For 1 Star Block D (Cut 3 total.)

From one gray or cream batik, cut:
4 squares, 3⅛" x 3⅛"; cut in half diagonally to yield 8 half-square triangles

From a second gray or cream batik, cut:
4 squares, 3⅛" x 3⅛"; cut in half diagonally to yield 8 half-square triangles

Block A Assembly

1 With a pencil and ruler, draw a diagonal line from corner to corner on the wrong side of the gray or cream 3⅞" squares. Place a marked square on a navy-blue tree-print 3⅞" square, right sides together. Sew ¼" from the drawn line on both sides. Cut on the drawn line. Press the seam allowances toward the navy-blue halves. Make four half-square-triangle units.

Make 4
per block.

2 Arrange the units from step 1, a gray or cream 3½" square, and four navy-blue 3½" squares as shown. Sew the pieces together into rows; press the seam allowances as shown. Sew the rows together; press the seam allowances toward the center. Make three blocks.

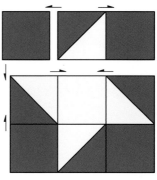

Block A.
Make 3.

Star Block B Assembly

1 Sew a gray or cream quarter-square triangle to a navy-blue quarter-square triangle as shown. Press the seam allowances toward the blue. Then add a gray or cream half-square triangle as shown; press the seam allowances toward the half-square triangle. Make four units.

Make 4
per block.

2 Arrange the units from step 1, the gray or cream 3½" square, and four navy-blue 3½" squares as shown. Sew the pieces together into three rows; press the seam allowances as shown. Sew the rows together and press toward the center. Make four blocks.

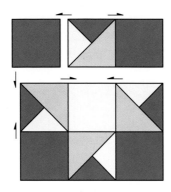

Block B.
Make 4.

Star Block C Assembly

1 Using two quarter-square triangles of one gray or cream batik, a quarter-square triangle of the second gray or cream batik, and a navy-blue quarter-square triangle, sew the triangles together in pairs as shown. Press and sew the pairs together. Split the seam as shown in the "Helpful Hint for Flat Seams" on page 13 and press. Make four of these units.

Make 4.

2 Arrange the units from step 1, the gray or cream 3½" square, and four navy-blue 3½" squares as shown. Sew the pieces together into three rows. Press the seam allowances as shown. Sew the rows together

and press the seam allowances toward the center. Make four blocks.

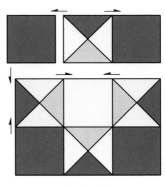

Block C.
Make 4.

Star Block D Assembly

1 Using the half-square triangles, sew together two triangles of different cream or gray fabrics as shown to make unit A. Sew cream or gray triangles to navy-blue triangles as shown to make units B and C. Press the seam allowances toward the navy blue fabric. Make four of each unit.

Unit A.   Unit B.   Unit C.
Make 4 of each.

2 Arrange the units with four navy-blue 2¾" squares as shown. Sew the pieces together into pairs; press. Then sew the pairs together into quarters. Refer to the "Helpful Hint for Flat Seams" to split the seam for pressing. Sew the top and the bottom quarters together; press the seam allowances toward the navy-blue squares. Sew the two halves together to complete the block. Make three blocks.

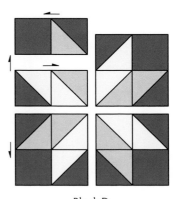

Block D.
Make 3.

Sashing and Inner Border Assembly

1 Using a pencil and ruler, draw a diagonal line from corner to corner on the wrong side of each light-blue tone-on-tone 1½" square. Place a marked square on one corner of a cream polka-dot 2½" x 9½" rectangle, right sides together, as shown. Sew on the drawn line. Trim the seam allowances to ¼"; press the seam allowances toward the triangle. Repeat to sew a square on each corner of the cream polka-dot rectangle. Make 82 sashing rectangles.

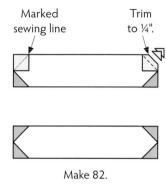

Marked sewing line   Trim to ¼".

Make 82.

2 Draw a diagonal line from corner to corner on the wrong side of each light-blue tone-on-tone 1⅞" square. Lay two marked squares on opposite corners of a navy-blue 3¼" square. Sew ¼" from the drawn line on both sides. Cut on the drawn line; press.

No-Mark Sewing on the Diagonal

When sewing a lot of squares on the diagonal, I find it useful to make a guide on the bed of my sewing machine with tape. Use a straight edge in line with the needle to position the tape. Then, instead of drawing a line on the back of each square with a pencil, you can guide the corner of the square along the edge of the tape.

3 Lay a marked light-blue 1⅞" square on the navy-blue corner of each half from step 2 as shown. Sew ¼" from the drawn line on both sides. Cut on the drawn line; press. This will give you four flying-geese units. Make a total of 28 flying-geese units.

Make 28.

4 Arrange six of the units from step 3 and five navy-blue 1½" x 9½" rectangles as shown. Sew the pieces together; press the seam allowances toward the navy-blue rectangles. Make two of these border strips for the top and bottom of the quilt. Then arrange eight of the units from step 3, seven navy-blue 1½" x 9½" rectangles, and two navy-blue 1½" squares as shown. Sew the pieces together; press the seam allowances toward the navy-blue pieces. Make two border strips for the sides of the quilt.

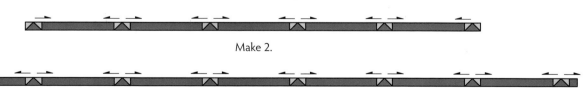

Make 2.

Make 2.

Quilt-Top Assembly

1 Arrange the pieced blocks, the navy-blue 9½" squares, the sashing rectangles, and the 2½" sashing squares as shown in the quilt assembly diagram below. Place the assorted gray or cream sashing squares randomly in the sashing rows. See the photo on page 42 for placement guidance.

2 Sew the blocks and sashing rectangles together in horizontal rows. Press the seam allowances toward the blocks. Sew the sashing rectangles and squares together in horizontal rows. Press the seam allowances toward the sashing squares.

3 Sew the sashing rows and block rows together; press the seam allowances in one direction. The quilt top should measure 57½" x 79½".

4 Sew the top and bottom pieced borders to the quilt; press the seam allowances toward the borders. Sew the pieced side borders to the quilt; press the seam allowances toward the borders.

5 Measure the length of the quilt through the center and trim the navy-blue 4½" x 83" outer-border strips to that length. Sew them to the sides of the quilt; press the seam allowances outward.

6 Sew the four navy-blue 4½" x 42" strips together end to end to make one long strip. Measure the width of the quilt through the center, including the borders just added. Cut two strips to that length and sew them to the top and bottom of the quilt; press the seam allowances toward the outer border.

Finishing the Quilt

1 Prepare the backing fabric. Layer the backing, batting, and quilt top. Baste the layers together, and hand or machine quilt as desired. (If you are taking your quilt to a long-arm quilter, you don't need to baste the layers together.)

2 Cut and prepare approximately 330" of 2¼"-wide bias binding using the dark-blue batik. Sew the binding to the quilt.

Quilt assembly

Pink of Perfection

Materials

Yardage is based on 42"-wide fabric. Fat quarters measure 18" x 21".

2¼ yards of pink-and-red leaf-print batik for setting blocks, setting triangles, and outer border

⅔ yard of pink batik for blocks

⅓ yard of burgundy-and-pink batik for inner border

1 fat quarter *each* of 6 or 7 assorted pink, burgundy, and red batiks for blocks

¾ yard of burgundy batik for binding

3⅓ yards of fabric for backing

55" x 69" piece of batting

Cutting

All measurements include ¼"-wide seam allowances.

From the assorted pink, burgundy, and red fat quarters, cut a *total* of:
36 strips, 1½" x 21"

From the pink batik, cut:
2 strips, 6½" x 42"; crosscut into 12 squares, 6½" x 6½"
3 strips, 2½" x 42"; crosscut into 48 squares, 2½" x 2½"

From the pink-and-red leaf-print batik, cut:
2 strips, 10½" x 42"; crosscut into 6 squares, 10½" x 10½"
3 squares, 15½" x 15½"; cut into quarters diagonally to yield 12 quarter-square triangles (2 are extra)
2 squares, 8" x 8"; cut in half diagonally to yield 4 half-square triangles
6 strips, 3½" x 42"

From the burgundy-and-pink batik, cut:
6 strips, 1½" x 42"

Block Assembly

1 Sew together six assorted pink, burgundy, and red 1½" x 21" strips along their long edges to make a strip set; press. Make six strip sets. Crosscut the strip sets into 48 segments, 2½" wide.

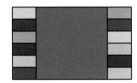

Make 6 strip sets.
Cut 48 segments.

2 Sew segments from step 1 to opposite sides of a pink 6½" square to make a center unit; press. Make 12 center units.

Make 12.

3 Sew a pink 2½" square to each end of a segment from step 1 as shown. Make 24 units; press.

Make 24.

4 Sew units from step 3 to the top and bottom of the center units from step 2 as shown; press. Make 12 blocks.

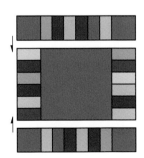

Make 12.

Quilt Top Assembly

1 Arrange the blocks, the pink-and-red leaf-print 10½" squares, and the setting triangles in diagonal rows as shown in the quilt assembly diagram below.

2 Sew the pieces together into diagonal rows. Press the seam allowances toward the pink-and-red squares. Sew the rows together, adding the corner triangles last; press.

3 Sew the burgundy-and-pink 1½"-wide strips together end to end to make one long strip. Measure the length of the quilt through the center and cut two strips to that length. Sew the strips to the sides of the quilt and press seam allowances toward the inner border. Measure the width of the quilt, including the borders just added, and cut two strips to that length. Sew them to the top and bottom of the quilt and press.

4 Repeat step 3 using the pink-and-red leaf-print 3½"-wide strips. Press the seam allowances toward the inner border.

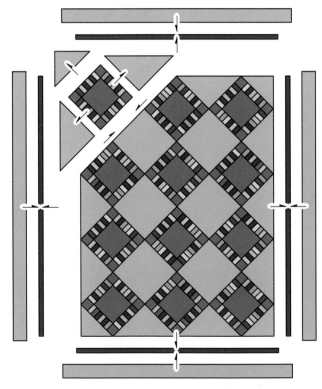

Quilt assembly

Finishing the Quilt

1 Prepare the backing fabric. Layer the backing, batting, and quilt top. Baste the layers together, and hand or machine quilt as desired. (If you are taking your quilt to a long-arm quilter, you don't need to baste the layers together.)

2 Cut and prepare approximately 250" of 2¼"-wide bias binding using the burgundy batik. Sew the binding to the quilt.

Quilting Suggestions

I quilted a "funky feather" in the border and a circular version of the feather in the open squares and triangles. The blocks are quilted with a continuous-line design.

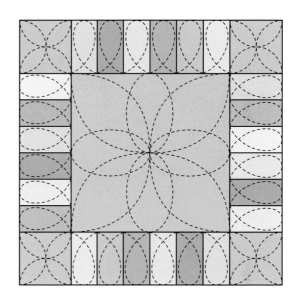

Finished Quilt: 51½" x 63½"

Simply Irresistible

Materials

Yardage is based on 42"-wide fabric. Fat quarters measure 18" x 21".

1⅝ yards of bright batik for outer border

1⅛ yards of black batik for sashing, sashing squares, and inner border

⅝ yard of red-and-orange batik for sashing and sashing squares

1 fat quarter *each* of 11 assorted batiks for blocks*

¾ yard of black batik for binding

3¼ yards of fabric for backing

56" x 68" piece of batting

* You could also use 11 precut 10" squares, such as Moda Layer Cake squares.

Cutting

All measurements include ¼"-wide seam allowances.

From the black batik, cut:

23 strips, 1½" x 42"; crosscut *1 strip* into 22 squares, 1½" x 1½"

From the red-and-orange batik, cut:

13 strips, 1½" x 42"

From *each* of the 11 assorted batik fat quarters, cut:

1 square, 9½" x 9½"

From the bright batik, cut:

1 square, 9½" x 9½"

6 strips, 4½" x 42"

11 strips, 1½" x 42"; crosscut:

5 strips into 14 rectangles, 1½" x 11½"

4 strips into 14 rectangles, 1½" x 9½"

1 strip into 8 rectangles, 1½" x 2½", and 4 squares, 1½" x 1½"

Strip Set Assembly

You will make strip sets and cut segments to make the sashing, sashing blocks, and pieced inner borders.

1 Sew a black 1½"-wide strip to each long edge of a red-and-orange 1½"-wide strip to make strip set A. Press the seam allowances toward the black fabric. Make eight strip sets. Crosscut the strip sets into a total of 31 segments, 9½" wide.

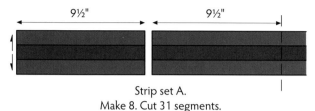

Strip set A.
Make 8. Cut 31 segments.

2 Sew a red-and-orange 1½"-wide strip to each long edge of a black 1½"-wide strip to make strip set B. Press the seam allowances toward the black fabric. Make two strip sets. Crosscut the strip sets into 40 segments, 1½" wide.

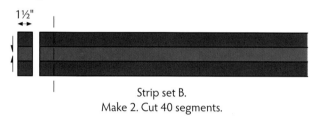

Strip set B.
Make 2. Cut 40 segments.

3 Sew a black 1½"-wide strip to each long edge of a red-and-orange 1½"-wide strip to make strip set C. Press the seam allowances toward the black fabric. Crosscut the strip sets into 20 segments, 1½" wide.

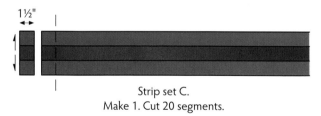

Strip set C.
Make 1. Cut 20 segments.

4 Arrange two B segments and one C segment as shown. Sew the segments together to make a sashing block; press the seam allowances toward the center. Make 20 sashing blocks.

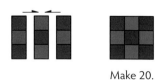

Make 20.

Quilt Top Assembly

1 Arrange the 11 assorted 9½" squares and one bright 9½" square as desired. See the photo on page 52 for color-placement guidance. Sew a sashing segment to the top edge of each square, and then sew a sashing segment to the bottom edge of the three blocks in the bottom row as shown. Sew the squares together to make three vertical rows; press the seam allowances toward the sashing strips.

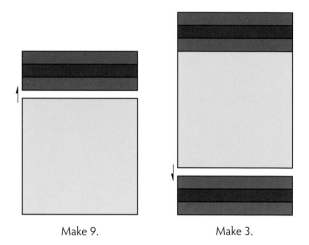

Make 9.   Make 3.

2 Sew a sashing square to the top of each remaining sashing strip; then sew a sashing square to the bottom of four of these strips. Sew the strips together to make four vertical rows; press the seam allowances toward the sashing strips.

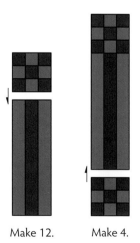

Make 12.   Make 4.

3 Referring to the quilt assembly diagram on the facing page, sew the vertical rows together. The quilt should measure 39½" x 51½".

Borders

1 Sew a black 1½"-wide strip to each long edge of a bright 1½"-wide strip to make strip set D. Press the seam allowances toward the black fabric. Crosscut the strip set into 18 segments, 1½" wide.

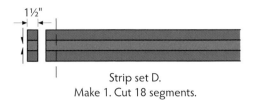

Strip set D.
Make 1. Cut 18 segments.

2 For the top and bottom first inner borders, sew together four of the strip set D segments and three bright 1½" x 9½" rectangles as shown; press. Make two.

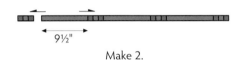

9½"

Make 2.

3 For the side first inner border, sew together two bright 1½" squares, five strip set D segments, and four bright 1½" x 9½" rectangles as shown; press. Make two.

9½"

Make 2.

4 Sew the top and bottom border strips and then the side border strips to the quilt. Press toward the inner borders.

5 For the top and bottom second inner borders, sew together two bright 1½" x 2½" rectangles, four black 1½" squares, and three bright 1½" x 11½" rectangles as shown; press. Make two.

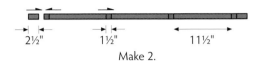

2½"   1½"   11½"

Make 2.

6 For the side second inner border, sew together seven black 1½" squares, two bright 1½" x 2½" rectangles, and four bright 1½" x 11½" rectangles as shown; press. Make two.

2½"   1½"   11½"

Make 2.

7 Sew the top and bottom border strips and then the side border strips to the quilt.

8 Sew the bright 4½"-wide strips together end to end to make one long strip. Measure, cut, and sew the strips to the top and bottom of the quilt, and then to the sides of the quilt for the outer border.

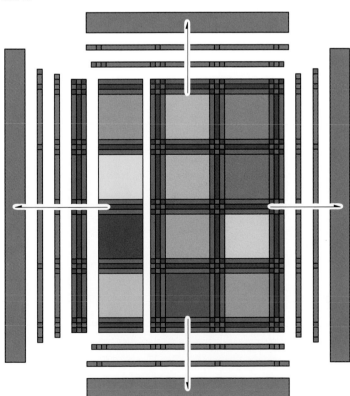

Quilt assembly

Finishing the Quilt

1 Prepare the backing fabric. Layer the backing, batting, and quilt top. Baste the layers together, and hand or machine quilt as desired. (If you are taking your quilt to a long-arm quilter, you don't need to baste the layers together.)

2 Cut and prepare approximately 235" of 2¼"-wide bias binding using the black batik. Sew the binding to the quilt.

Quilting Suggestions

I quilted a pointy feather motif in the border, and then used the same feather motif in a medallion design within each block. I stitched in the ditch of the sashing and inner borders.

Power to the People

Materials

Yardage is based on 42"-wide fabric. Fat quarters measure 18" x 21".

2¼ yards of mottled cream batik for blocks and inner border

1¼ yards of pink-and-blue leaf-print batik for outer border

1 fat quarter *each* of 16 assorted bright batiks for blocks and setting triangles

⅔ yard of purple tone-on-tone batik for binding

3⅞ yards of fabric for backing

68" x 68" piece of batting

Marking pencil

Cutting

All measurements include ¼"-wide seam allowances.

From the mottled cream batik, cut:

10 strips, 4½" x 42"; crosscut into 80 squares, 4½" x 4½"*

8 strips, 2½" x 42"; crosscut into 64 rectangles, 2½" x 4½"*

6 strips, 1½" x 42"

From *each* of the assorted bright fat quarters, cut:

4 squares, 3½" x 3½"*

4 rectangles, 2¼" x 4½"*

From the remainder of the assorted bright fat quarters, cut a *total* of:

13 pieces using the template on page 63 (9 for blocks, 4 for corner blocks)

31 to 35 strips, 3" x 21"* (27 to 30 for blocks, 4 or 5 for corner triangles)

3 different squares, 5¾" x 5¾"*; cut into quarters diagonally to make 12 quarter-square triangles

24 strips, 2¾" x 21"*

2 different squares, 3½" x 3½"; cut in half diagonally to make 4 half-square triangles

From the pink-and-blue leaf-print batik, cut:

6 strips, 5½" x 42"

2 strips, 2½" x 42"; crosscut into 8 squares, 2½" x 2½"*, and 8 rectangles, 2½" x 6"*

* *Because these pieces will be trimmed as you construct the blocks, the cutting does not need to be as exact as for normal piecing.*

Finished Quilt: 63" x 63" | Finished Blocks: 9" x 9"

A Note about the Blocks

The blocks and setting triangles in the quilt shown were pieced on a foundation. Because there's not enough space in this book to include the patterns, the cutting and step-by-step instructions are written for more freeform, random piecing. Your blocks will look slightly different from those in the quilt shown, and they will all be slightly different from each other. Some of the triangle points may be cut off when blocks are trimmed to size. This will make your quilt unique, spontaneous, and whimsical. However, if you would like to use foundation piecing for your blocks, please visit the publisher's website (ShopMartingale.com) where you can download the patterns for both blocks, the side setting triangles, and the corner setting triangles.

Block A Assembly

1 Trim a mottled cream 4½" square at random angles as shown to make a block center. Take off a total of about ½" so that the center is roughly 4" x 4". Sew matching bright 2¼" x 4½" rectangles to the sides of the block center. Press. Trim the bright rectangles at random angles.

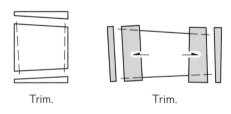

Trim.   Trim.

2 Sew a mottled cream 2½" x 4½" rectangle to each side of the unit from step 1. Press and trim the top and bottom of this unit to align with the angle of the block center.

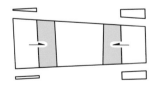

3 Sew a mottled cream 2½" x 4½" rectangle to a bright 2¼" x 4½" rectangle. Trim the bright piece at a random angle. Trim the sides of this unit to be ½" larger than the top of the block center from step 2. Make a dot in the seam allowance of the top unit and the block center so that you can match them up correctly later. Make a second unit for the bottom in the same manner, trimming the sides to be ½" larger than the bottom of the block center. Leave the bottom piece unmarked.

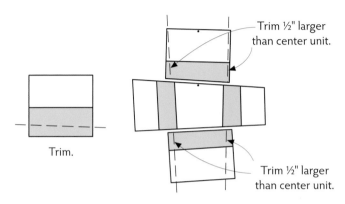

Trim ½" larger than center unit.

Trim.

Trim ½" larger than center unit.

4 Using a pencil and ruler, draw a diagonal line from corner to corner on the wrong side of four bright 3½" squares. Lay a marked square on one corner of a mottled cream 4½" square, right sides together. Sew on the drawn line. Cut away the corner, leaving a ¼" seam allowance. Press toward the bright triangle. Repeat to make a total of four corner units.

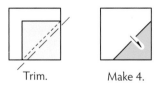

Trim.   Make 4.

5 Sew a corner unit to each side of the units made in step 3. Press and trim the units to make a straight edge, following the line of the center unit.

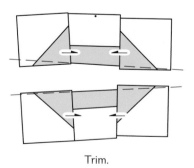

Trim.

6 Sew the top and bottom units to the center unit, matching the seams of the block center. Don't worry if they don't match exactly. This is a wonky block, after all! Press and trim the entire block to 9½" x 9½". Some of the triangle points may be cut off, but that's OK! Make 16 blocks.

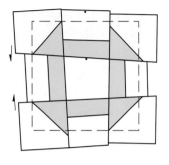

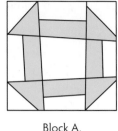

Block A.
Make 16.

Block B Assembly

For each block, you'll need one bright batik piece cut using the center block template, one 3" x 21" strip of a second bright batik, and two 3" x 21" strips of a third bright batik.

1 Roughly cut two squares from the second bright batik strip. Sew a square to each side of the center piece; press and trim to align with the angle of the center piece.

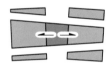

2 Place the remainder of the bright strip along one edge of the center unit and sew. Trim and press. Sew the remainder of the strip to the opposite side of the block, trim, and press. Trim the block edges at random angles.

Trim.

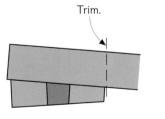
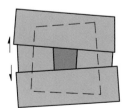

3 Sew a strip of the third bright batik to each side of the block; press and trim to the center angles.

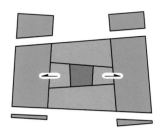

4 Sew the remainder of the strips to the top and bottom of the block; press. Trim the block to 9½" x 9½" square. Make nine blocks.

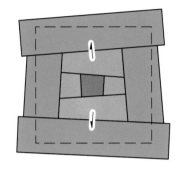
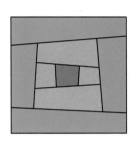

Block B.
Make 9.

Side Setting Triangle Assembly

For each side setting triangle, you will need one bright batik quarter-square triangle, one 2¾" x 21" strip of a second bright batik, and one 2¾" x 21" strip of a third bright batik.

1 Trim one side of the triangle to create a sharper angle at the point. Place a 2¾"-wide batik strip along the right side of the triangle, right sides together, with the end of the strip at the point of the triangle. Sew, press, and trim the strip to match the center.

2 Sew the remainder of the strip to the left side of the triangle; press. Trim the strip even with the center triangle. Then trim the outer edges of the triangle as shown.

3 Sew the third batik strip to the right side of the triangle as before; press and trim to match the angle of the center. Sew the remainder of the strip to the left side of the triangle; press and trim the strip.

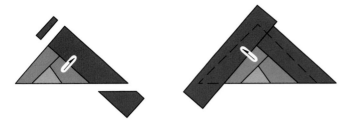

4 Press and trim the entire triangle so that the bottom of the triangle measures 14" and there is a 90° angle at the top. The sides should measure just slightly longer than 10¾". Make 12 side setting triangles.

Side Setting Triangle.
Make 12.

Corner Setting Triangle Assembly

For each corner setting triangle, you will need one bright batik half-square triangle, one 3"-wide strip at least 8" long of a second bright batik, and one 3"-wide strip at least 10½" long of a third bright batik.

1 Trim the long edge of a bright triangle at a random angle as shown. Sew a 3" x 8" batik strip to the triangle, centering it along the long side. Press and trim the long edge of the strip at a random angle.

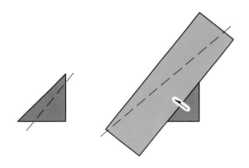

2 Add the 3" x 10½" batik strip, centering it on the long edge of the triangle; press. Trim the triangle so that the two shorter sides both measure 7¼", making sure that the corner is an accurate 90° angle. Make four corner setting triangles.

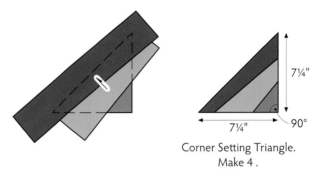

Corner Setting Triangle.
Make 4 .

Border Corner Block Assembly

For each block you will need one bright batik piece cut using the template, two pink-and-blue leaf-print 2½" squares, and two pink-and-blue leaf-print 2½" x 6" rectangles.

1 Sew a pink-blue leaf-print square to each side of the template piece; press and trim to the angle of the center.

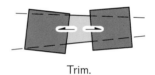

Trim.

2 Sew pink-and-blue leaf-print 2½" x 6" rectangles to the top and bottom of the unit; press. Trim the block to 5½" x 5½" square. Make four blocks.

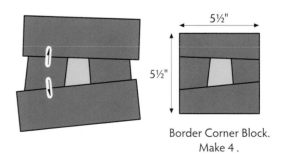

Border Corner Block.
Make 4 .

Quilt Top Assembly

1 Arrange the A and B blocks and the setting triangles in diagonal rows as shown in the quilt assembly diagram below. Rotate the blocks so that the angles go in different directions, referring to the photo on page 58 for placement guidance.

2 Sew the pieces together into diagonal rows. Press the seam allowances toward the B blocks. Sew the rows together, adding the corner triangles last; press.

3 Sew the mottled cream 1½"-wide strips together end to end to make one long strip. Measure the width of the quilt through the center and cut two strips to that length. Sew the strips to the top and bottom of the quilt and press the seam allowances toward the inner border. Measure the length of the quilt through the center, including the borders just added. Cut two strips to that length and sew them to the sides of the quilt. Press.

4 Sew the pink-and-blue leaf-print 5½"-wide strips together end to end to make one long strip. Measure as before and cut four borders to the measured length. Sew the strips to the sides of the quilt; press toward the inner border.

5 Sew a corner block to each end of the two remaining border strips. Press the seam allowances toward the corner blocks. Sew the borders to the top and bottom of the quilt and press.

Finishing the Quilt

1 Prepare the backing fabric. Layer the backing, batting, and quilt top. Baste the layers together, and hand or machine quilt as desired. (If you are taking your quilt to a long-arm quilter, you don't need to baste the layers together.)

2 Cut and prepare approximately 270" of 2¼"-wide bias binding using the purple tone-on-tone batik. Sew the binding to the quilt.

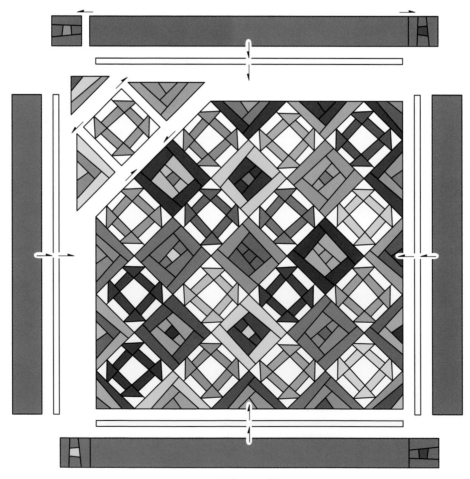

Quilt assembly

Quilting Suggestions

I machine quilted a "marshmallow" feather motif in the outer border, and in the center I quilted an allover pattern mixing "marshmallow" swirl sections with more angular areas.

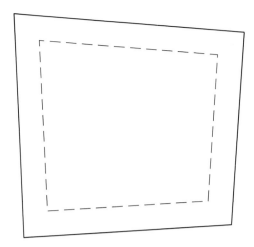

Center Block B and
Corner blocks

Finished Quilt: 57½" x 61½"

Night and Day

Night or day, this quilt will bring a smile to your heart. It started as a quilt designed on computer by my talented husband, Neil, and from there it took on a life of its own!

Materials

Yardages are based on 42"-wide fabric. Fat quarters measure 18" x 21".

1⅛ yards of dark-blue batik for outer border

½ yard of yellow batik for sun face appliqué and pieced border

½ yard of light-orange batik for sunray appliqué and pieced border

1 fat quarter *each* of 7 or 8 assorted dark-blue to purple batiks for background and moon appliqué

1 fat quarter *each* of 5 or 6 assorted light-blue to aqua batiks for background and star appliqués

1 fat quarter *each* of 4 assorted yellow to orange batiks for appliqués and pieced border

1 fat quarter of red-and-orange batik for appliqués and pieced border

⅔ yard of dark-blue batik for binding

3¾ yards of fabric for backing

62" x 66" piece of batting

Freezer paper for appliqué

Cutting

All measurements include ¼"-wide seam allowances.

From the assorted dark-blue to purple fat quarters, cut a *total* of:

42 rectangles, 4½" x 6½"

4 squares, 4½" x 4½"

5 rectangles, 2¾" x 5⅜"

4 rectangles, 2½" x 4½"

From the assorted light-blue to aqua fat quarters, cut a *total* of:

34 rectangles, 4½" x 6½"

4 squares, 4½" x 4½"

5 rectangles, 2¾" x 5⅜"

6 rectangles, 2½" x 4½"

From the dark-blue batik, cut:

7 strips, 5" x 42"

Appliqué Background Assembly

1 Layer the five dark 2¾" x 5⅜" rectangles all right side up. Cut the stack of rectangles in half diagonally, cutting from bottom left to top right as shown. Repeat for the five light 2¾" x 5⅜" rectangles. Pair each light rectangle with a dark rectangle, right sides together, and stitch them together along their long diagonal edges. (Notice that the points extend ¾" beyond the ends of the opposite-color triangle.) Press the triangles open and trim the long points even with the edge of the unit, which should measure 2½" x 4½". Make 10 units.

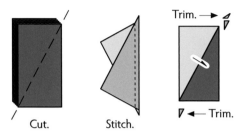

2 Lay out the light-blue to aqua rectangles and squares, the dark-blue to purple rectangles and squares, and the pieced rectangles as shown, placing the lightest rectangles in the center and transitioning to darker shades along the outer edges and corners. Refer to the photo on page 64 for color-placement guidance. Sew the rectangles and squares into horizontal rows and press the seam allowances in opposite directions from row to row. Sew the rows together and press. The quilt top should measure 44½" x 48½".

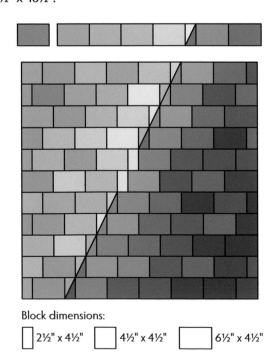

Block dimensions:

☐ 2½" x 4½"   ☐ 4½" x 4½"   ☐ 6½" x 4½"

Appliqué

The instructions are written for hand appliqué, but you can use your own favorite method if you prefer.

1 Using the patterns on pages 69–75, join patterns as noted and then trace each appliqué shape onto the dull side of freezer paper and cut out the templates on the drawn line.

2 Prepare the appliqués by pressing the freezer-paper templates shiny side down onto the right side of the chosen appliqué fabrics. Trace and cut out each appliqué shape, adding a scant ¼" seam allowance around the marked lines. The traced line will be your stitching line. Gently peel the freezer paper off the fabric.

3 The appliqué will be done in layers, in numerical order. Appliqué eye and mouth pieces 1 and 2 to the dark face piece 3. Then appliqué eye and mouth pieces 4 and 5 to the light face piece 6. Align the eye and mouth pieces and appliqué piece 3 to piece 6.

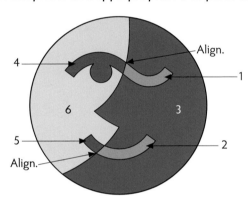

4 Position piece 7 onto the pieced background, aligning the outside edge points with the angled line of the background half rectangles, and centering the entire design within the background. (See photo on page 64 for placement.) Stitch along the outer curved edge and the short side edges, leaving the inner curve unsewn.

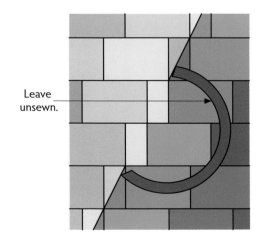

5 Appliqué the entire face in place, covering the raw edge of piece 7.

6 Appliqué five sunray shapes (piece 8) onto sunray piece 10. Then, appliqué the pointed side of sunray piece 9 onto the piece 10. Appliqué the entire sunray unit to the pieced background, aligning the inside edge points with the angled line of the background half rectangles. Refer to the photo on page 64 for placement guidance.

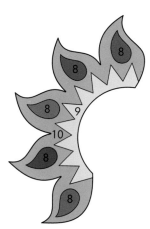

7 Appliqué the 10 triangles (piece 11) and 5 stars (piece 12), referring to the photo for placement guidance.

8 From the wrong side, cut away the pieced background behind the face and behind the sunrays, leaving a ¼" seam allowance.

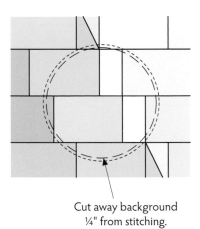

Cut away background ¼" from stitching.

Inner Border Assembly

The inner borders are pieced on a paper foundation. Paper piecing is a great way to piece shapes with odd angles or sharp points. All fabric is placed on the blank (unmarked) side of the foundation pattern. Fabric pieces are sewn to the foundation paper in numerical order.

1 Make 24 copies of the inner-border pattern on page 69. To ensure accuracy, make all photocopies for your quilt project on the same copy machine. If you prefer, you can also trace the pattern directly onto paper made specifically for foundation piecing. The marked lines will be your sewing lines.

2 For each inner-border piece, cut seven strips, approximately 2½" wide, of assorted yellow and orange fabrics. Place the first fabric piece on the unmarked side of the foundation paper, right side up over area 1. Hold the fabric and foundation paper up to the light to make sure that area 1 is completely covered and includes an ample seam allowance.

3 Place fabric piece 2 on top of piece 1, right sides together. Hold the pieces up to the light to make sure that at least ¼" of fabric extends over the line separating areas 1 and 2.

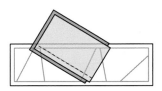

4 Set your sewing machine's stitch length to between 15 and 20 stitches per inch. Holding the layers firmly in place, turn the foundation over, and carefully position the unit under the presser foot, paper side up. Sew on the line between areas 1 and 2, stitching into the ¼" outer seam allowance on the block.

5 Trim seam allowances to ¼" wide, being careful not to cut the foundation paper. Flip open piece 2 and press the fabric into place with a dry iron.

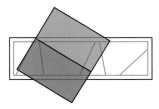

6 Continue sewing the pieces to the foundation paper in numerical order until the border unit is complete.

7 Trim away the excess fabric around the edges of the block, being sure to leave a ¼" seam allowance. Press.

8 Repeat the steps to make 24 border units. It's a good idea to keep the foundation paper in place until after the quilt top is assembled.

Quilt Top Assembly

1 Sew six border units together end to end. Make two for the side borders and sew them to the quilt top. Press the seam allowances toward the quilt top.

2 Sew six border units together end to end. Make two for the top and bottom borders and sew them to the quilt top. Press the seam allowances toward the quilt top.

3 Sew the dark-blue 5"-wide strips together end to end to make one long strip. Cut two strips, 57½" long, for the top and bottom borders and two strips, 61½" long, for the side borders.

4 To add the mitered borders, refer to page 14 for steps 6–8 of "Quilt Top Assembly" for the quilt "September." Sew the border strips to the top and bottom and then to the sides of the quilt. Miter each of the corners. Press the seam allowances toward the outer border.

5 Gently remove the paper foundations from the inner border.

6 Appliqué three stars (piece 12) in place in the upper-left corner of the outer border as shown in the photo on page 64. Appliqué the moon (piece 13) in place in the lower-right corner.

Finishing the Quilt

1 Prepare the backing fabric. Layer the backing, batting, and quilt top. Baste the layers together, and hand or machine quilt as desired. (If you are taking your quilt to a long-arm quilter, you don't need to baste the layers together.)

2 Cut and prepare approximately 250" of 2¼"-wide bias binding using the dark-blue batik. Sew the binding to the quilt.

Quilting Suggestions

I machine quilted the light side with a sunray pattern, and on the dark side I used more subdued horizontal lines to suggest a sunset-like motif. The inner border is quilted with a swirl design, and the outer border is quilted in a feather design that mimics the sunrays.

Quilt assembly

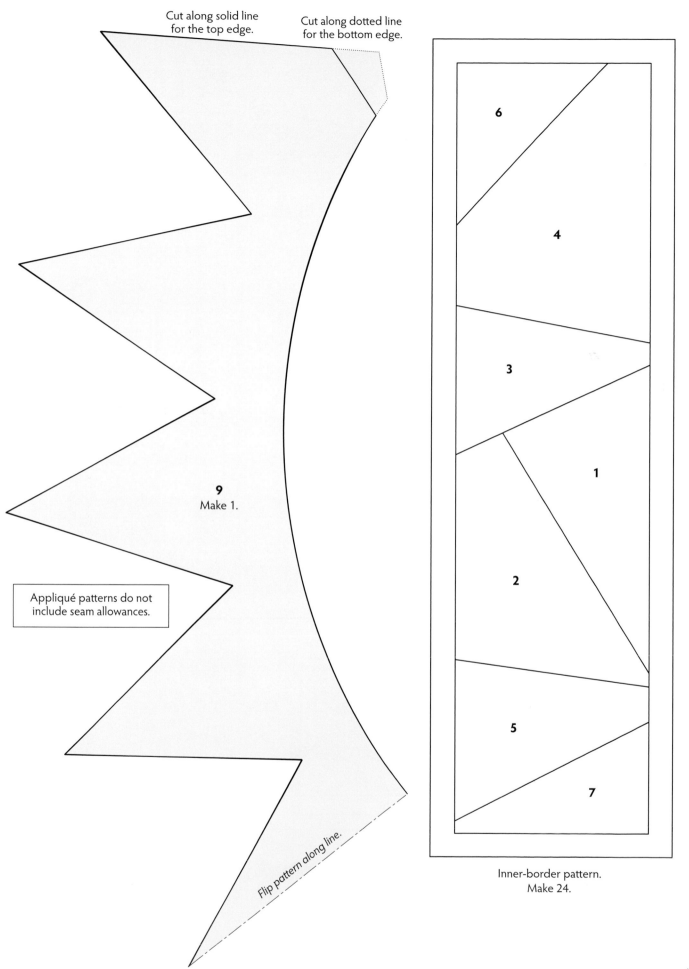

Cut along solid line
for the top edge.

Cut along dotted line
for the bottom edge.

9
Make 1.

Appliqué patterns do not
include seam allowances.

Flip pattern along line.

6

4

3

1

2

5

7

Inner-border pattern.
Make 24.

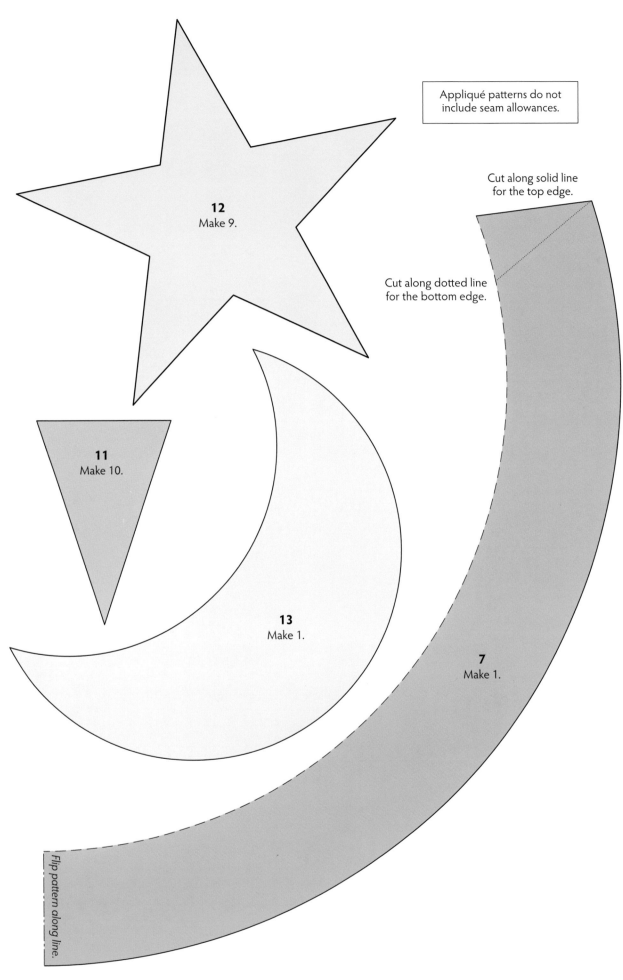

Appliqué patterns do not include seam allowances.

Cut along solid line for the top edge.

Cut along dotted line for the bottom edge.

12
Make 9.

11
Make 10.

13
Make 1.

7
Make 1.

Flip pattern along line.

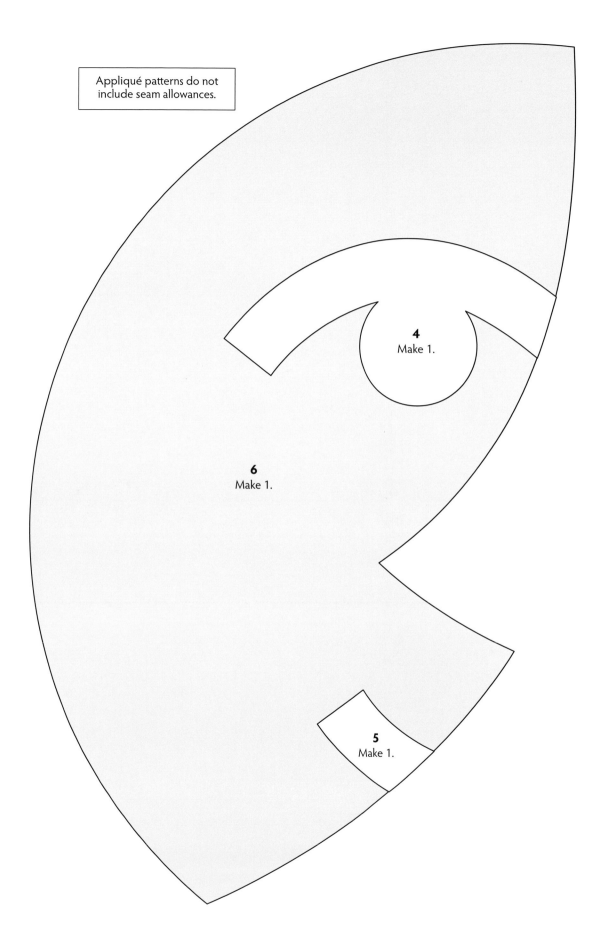

Appliqué patterns do not include seam allowances.

4
Make 1.

6
Make 1.

5
Make 1.

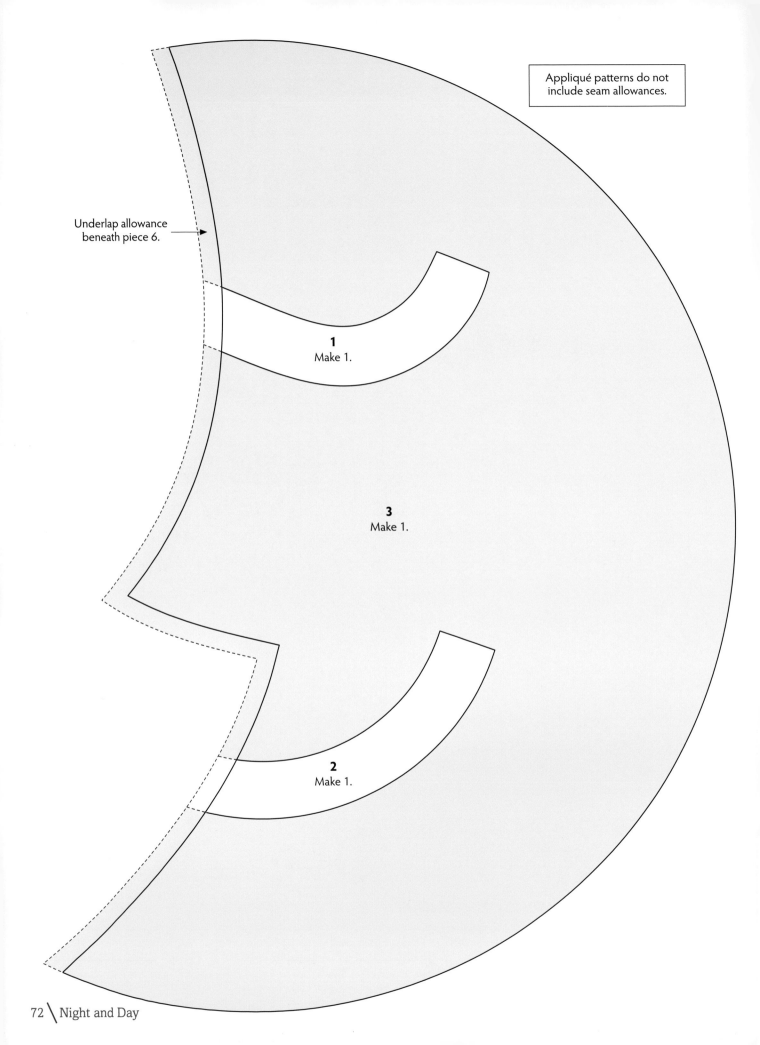

Appliqué patterns do not include seam allowances.

Underlap allowance beneath piece 6.

1
Make 1.

3
Make 1.

2
Make 1.

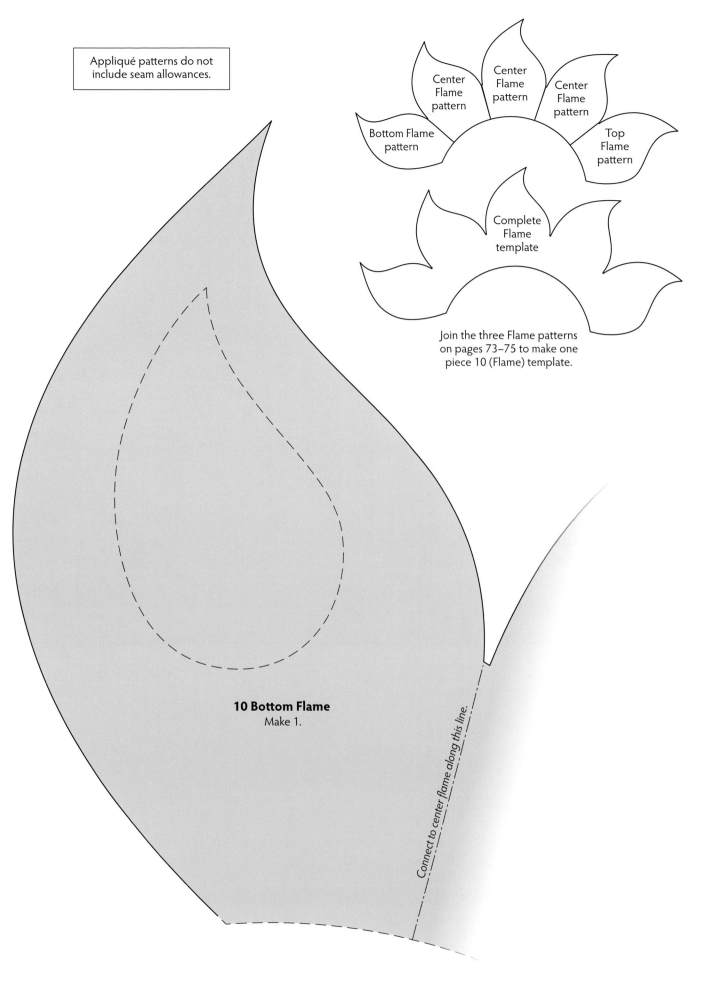

Appliqué patterns do not include seam allowances.

Center Flame pattern

Center Flame pattern

Center Flame pattern

Bottom Flame pattern

Top Flame pattern

Complete Flame template

Join the three Flame patterns on pages 73–75 to make one piece 10 (Flame) template.

10 Bottom Flame
Make 1.

Connect to center flame along this line.

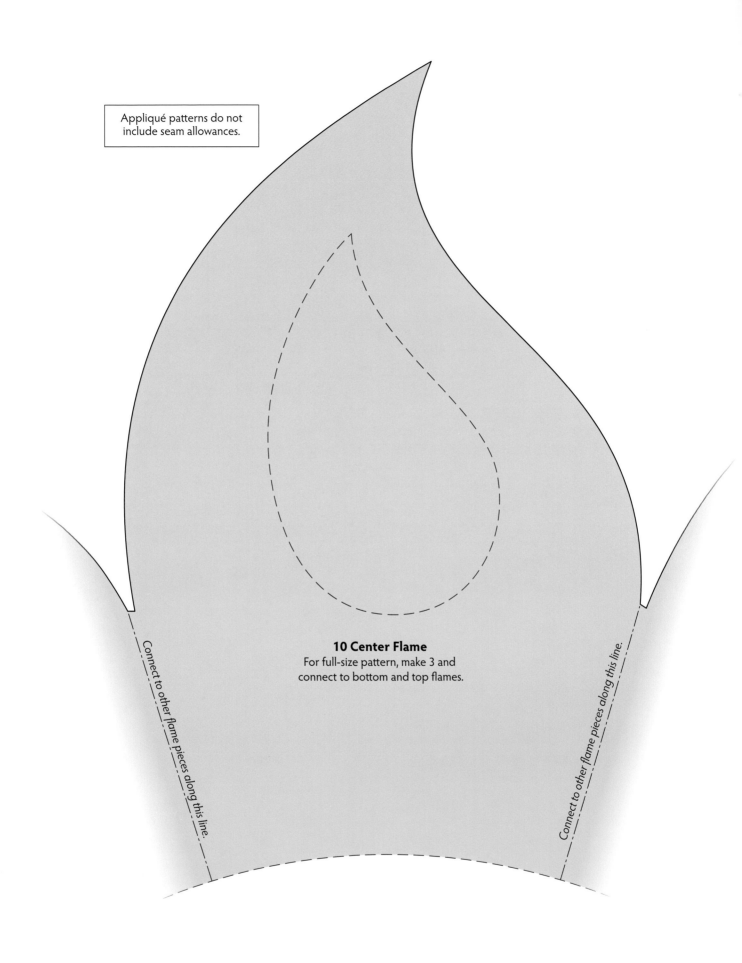

Appliqué patterns do not include seam allowances.

10 Center Flame
For full-size pattern, make 3 and connect to bottom and top flames.

Connect to other flame pieces along this line.

Connect to other flame pieces along this line.

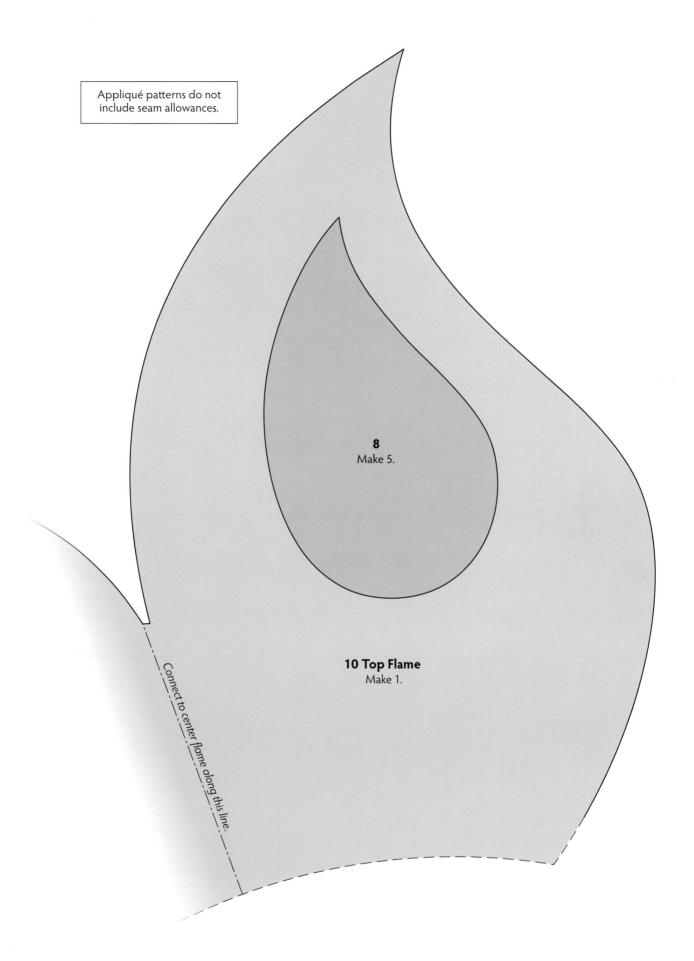

Appliqué patterns do not include seam allowances.

8
Make 5.

10 Top Flame
Make 1.

Connect to center flame along this line.

Finished Quilt: 52½" x 68½" | Finished Blocks: 6" x 6"

Paradise Winds

Materials

Yardage is based on 42"-wide fabric. Fat quarters measure 18" x 21".

1⅓ yards of green tone-on-tone batik for sashing

1⅛ yards of purple-and-teal batik for borders

1 fat quarter *each* of 6 or 7 assorted jewel-tone batiks (teal, green, and purple) for blocks

⅔ yard of purple batik for binding

3¼ yards of fabric for backing

57" x 73" piece of batting

Cutting

All measurements include ¼"-wide seam allowances.

From the assorted jewel-tone fat quarters, cut a *total* of:

24 strips, 3½" x 21"

From the green tone-on-tone batik, cut:

16 strips, 2½" x 42"; crosscut 7 strips into 40 rectangles, 2½" x 6½"

From the purple-and-teal batik, cut:

6 strips, 5½" x 42"

I love the combination of purple, teal, and green. There is something about it that makes me so happy! So take a trip to paradise with your batiks and this easy-to-piece quilt.

Block Assembly

1   Pairing up the colors randomly, sew two jewel-tone 3½" x 21" strips together along the long edges to make a strip set. Make 12 strip sets.

2   Cut the strip sets into 6½"-wide segments to make 35 blocks.

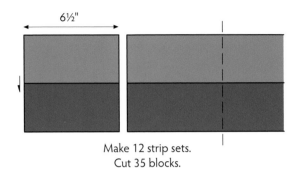

Make 12 strip sets.
Cut 35 blocks.

Quilt Top Assembly

1   Arrange the blocks in five vertical rows of seven blocks each, alternating the block orientation as shown in the photograph on page 76.

2   Sew a green tone-on-tone 2½" x 6½" rectangle to the top of each block. Sew the blocks together to form five vertical rows. Press seam allowances toward the green rectangles. Then sew a green tone-on-tone 2½" x 6½" rectangle to the bottom of each vertical row. Press.

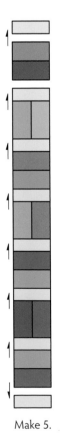

Make 5.

3   Measure the length of each vertical row. If the measurements differ, calculate the average and consider this the length. Sew the remaining green tone-on-tone strips together end to end to make one long strip. Cut six sashing strips to the averaged length. Sew a sashing strip to the right side of each vertical row. Sew the vertical rows together, and then sew the last sashing strip to the left side of the quilt.

Easy Alignment

When the vertical block rows and long sashing strips are sewn together, it's important for the short horizontal sashing strips to correctly line up on each side of the long sashing strip. Here's an easy way to mark the long strips. After sewing the strip to the side of a vertical row, simply clip the long sashing strip to show the junctions that must match. Be sure to clip only halfway (⅛") into the seam allowance. Then press the seam allowance toward the long sashing strip.

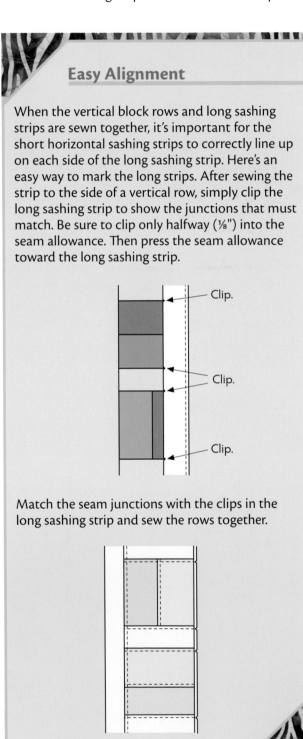

Match the seam junctions with the clips in the long sashing strip and sew the rows together.

4 Sew the purple-and-teal 5½"-wide strips together end to end to make one long strip. Measure the width of the quilt through the center and cut two strips to that length. Sew the strips to the top and bottom of the quilt. Press the seam allowances toward the border. Measure the length of the quilt through the center, including the borders just added. Cut two strips to that length and sew them to the sides of the quilt. Press.

Finishing the Quilt

1 Prepare the backing fabric. Layer the backing, batting, and quilt top. Baste the layers together, and hand or machine quilt as desired. (If you are taking your quilt to a long-arm quilter, you don't need to baste the layers together.)

2 Cut and prepare approximately 256" of 2¼"-wide bias binding using the purple batik. Sew the binding to the quilt.

Quilting Suggestions

I quilted a feather in the border and used the same feather and swirl, plus a paisley design, in the quilt center.

Quilt assembly

About the Author

Photo by Neil Brown

QuilterChic.com

Cheryl Brown started her creative life as a commercial interior designer; she enjoyed working with colors, textures, and fabric. She started quilting about 20 years ago, as a creative outlet when a sweet baby boy came into her family, and later a sweet baby girl.

For several years she worked at a local quilt shop, where she learned how to machine quilt. She bought her own long-arm machine and opened her business QuilterChic, in 2006, when she also started designing quilts. This is Cheryl's second book. Her first, *Fresh and Fabulous Quilts*, was also published by Martingale.

Cheryl lives in Centerville, Utah, with her husband, Neil, and her two children, Adrian and Natalie. She also has a diabetic cat, Daisy, who keeps life interesting!

Cheryl hosts a website that covers all things quilting. Check it out at quilterchic.com, or follow Cheryl on Facebook or Twitter.

Acknowledgments

I want to especially thank:

My wonderful husband, Neil, for his design skills, support, and love.

My two fun kids, who always believe in me.

My terrific sewing friends with their numerous offers of help. Also, my appliqué group, Snippets, for having endless patience with me.

My talented mother-in-law, Mary, for helping me learn how to quilt, and for sharing my love of all things quilting.